iMovie

User Guide

Transform Your Videos with Powerful Editing Tools From
Basic Cuts to Advanced Effects

Harper Quinn

Disclaimer and Terms of Use

The author and publisher of this book and the accompanying materials have used their best efforts in preparing this book. The author and publisher make no representation or warranties with respect to the accuracy, applicability, fitness, or completeness of the contents of this book. The information contained in this book is strictly for informational purposes. Therefore, if you wish to apply the ideas contained in this book, you are taking full responsibility for your actions.

Printed in the United States of America

TABLE OF CONTENTS

INTRODUCTION

In its most basic form, iMovie is an application for editing videos that was created by Apple Inc. As a component of the iLife suite of digital media software for Macintosh computers, it was first made available to the public in the year 1999. During the time since then, it has been through a great number of versions, each of which has improved and broadened its capabilities. It is now possible to use iMovie on iOS devices such as iPhones and iPads, in addition to being available on Mac computers. This makes it accessible to a wide range of people.

A user-friendly interface is one of the most enticing features of Apple's video editing software, iMovie. In addition to being aesthetically pleasing and user-friendly, the layout has a timeline at the bottom, which allows you to easily organize your clips, transitions, and effects. The interface may seem to be straightforward, but it conceals a wealth of capabilities that are hidden under the surface, just waiting to be found by editors with a sense of adventure. iMovie's ability to integrate without any problems with other Apple products and services is one of the program's defining characteristics. For instance, if you record video footage on your iPhone, you can effortlessly upload it to your Mac or iPad and continue editing from the point where you left off. This integrated environment helps to encourage a seamless and uninterrupted workflow, which enables you to concentrate on the creative process rather than becoming bogged down by technological obstacles.

On the other hand, iMovie is not just about ease; it is also about giving users more control. Everyone can become a storyteller using iMovie. You may use iMovie to bring your vision to life, whether you are filming a family trip, making a promotional video for your company, or aiming to become the next independent film phenomenon. iMovie gives you the tools you need to bring your vision to life. The large array of effects, transitions, and soundtracks that are already incorporated into iMovie is one of the most distinguishing characteristics of this program. The addition of a Hollywood-style flare to your projects may be accomplished with only a few clicks, transforming them from ordinary to remarkable outcomes. Are you interested in giving your video a retro vibe? What you're looking for is a filter. Want to make sure that the transitions between scenes are smooth? The large audio collection that is available with the software is the only place you need to look after. iMovie would be incomplete if it did not include powerful editing skills, and in this sense, it does not fall short of expectations. Whether you are cutting clips, altering audio levels, or performing color correction, iMovie gives you access to a full set of tools that you can use to fine-tune your masterpiece. Additionally, since it has a real-time preview option, you can see the impact of your adjustments immediately, which makes the editing process more iterative and responsive. However, the instructional potential of iMovie is possibly the most underappreciated feature of the program. iMovie is a video editing program that provides novices with a gentle introduction to the world of video editing. It does this by simplifying concepts such as timelines, transitions, and keyframes. When users reach a higher level of expertise, they can dig deeper into the advanced capabilities of iMovie, which allows them to strengthen their abilities and broaden their creative repertoire.

CHAPTER ONE
GETTING TO KNOW IMOVIE 2024

Overview

Chapter one talks about what iMovie is all about, how to understand iMovie, how to move around iMovie 2024 interface and so much more.

About iMovie

Apple, a technology powerhouse that is well-known for its cutting-edge products and elegant designs, has developed a video editing solution that is both powerful and easy to use. This solution is called iMovie. Apple, which has its headquarters in Cupertino, California, with offices located all over the world, has a long history of providing its devoted client base with new and innovative technological products. iMovie was developed to meet the requirements of people, small companies, and creative professionals who are looking for a video editing experience that is streamlined and easy to manipulate. The video-making iMovie is designed to assist organizations of all sizes in the process of browsing footage and creating films. To distribute personalized trailers across a variety of social media networks and websites, administrators may make use of the templates that are already built in. On a uniform interface, the system gives managers the ability to add titles, music, cast names, and transition effects across all of the graphics. Teams can use fonts, colors, gradients, patterns, and logos that are fully changeable with the use of iMovie. In addition, supervisors can choose tunes or include voice-overs for narration, cut video, add photographs, and apply filters to alter visual documents. Through the use of iMovie, companies can add effects such as split-screen, picture-in-picture, and green screen to movies that have been created in 4K quality on a centralized dashboard.

Even though iMovie is suited for users of all ability levels, the fact that it has a user interface that is easy to use and a complete set of capabilities makes it an excellent option for small to medium-sized enterprises, educational institutions, and creative firms. Whether you are a marketing professional who is generating appealing promotional films, a teacher who is creating engaging instructional material or a filmmaker who is bringing your creative vision to life, iMovie provides a strong toolbox that can improve your narrative. iMovie is a video editing program that enables users to easily create films of excellent quality. It is designed to meet the needs of a broad variety of businesses, including the media and entertainment industry, education, marketing, and creative services. iMovie is accessible on a wide range of devices, including Macs, iPads, and iPhones, thanks to its seamless integration into Apple's ecosystem. This makes it possible for you to edit and create motion pictures while you are on the go. iMovie is equipped with a complete set of functions that make the process of video editing much more straightforward. Apple's iMovie accelerates the creative process by providing a wide collection of built-in titles, transitions, and sound effects, as well as straightforward editing tools that allow users to drag and drop audio and video clips. In addition, it is compatible with a broad variety of video formats, which ensures that it is compatible with the media files that you already have.

Key Features and Modules of iMovie

Because of its extensive feature set, iMovie is a powerful video editing program that can accommodate both inexperienced and seasoned video editors.

The following is a list of some of the most important features and characteristics that make iMovie an exceptional option:

- **Magnetic Timeline**: The user-friendly Magnetic Timeline feature of iMovie makes it possible to effortlessly arrange and cut video segments, which in turn makes the editing process more streamlined and effective.
- **Advanced Editing Tools**: iMovie allows you to fine-tune your films to perfection by providing you with capabilities like a precision editor, green-screen effects, and advanced color correction.
- **Stunning Titles and Transitions**: Enhance your movies with a wide variety of titles, transitions, and motion graphics that can be customized to your liking, helping to ensure that your films have a polished and professional appearance.
- **Audio Editing**: The audio editing feature allows you to easily add voice overs, music tracks, and sound effects to your films. It also includes tools that allow you to change the levels and fade in and out of the audio.
- **Media Library Integration**: Streamline the creative process by allowing you to access and integrate material from your Photos and Music libraries in a seamless manner.
- **Sharing and Exporting**: You can share your masterpieces straight to prominent sites such as YouTube and Vimeo, as well as social media, or you can export them in a variety of formats for further dissemination.
- **iMovie Theater:** Use iMovie Theater to present your movies in a theatrical setting, complete with trailers, opening titles, and end credits. This feature allows you to showcase your films in a cinematic experience.

When it comes to video editing software, it is crucial to have features such as timelines that are easy to use, complex editing tools, and media integration that is seamlessly integrated. iMovie is a leading competitor in the market because it excels in these areas and provides users with a full set of features that make it easy for them to produce films that are of professional quality.

Pricing Options for iMovie: Adaptable and Easy to Access

With the implementation of a one-of-a-kind price plan for iMovie, Apple has made the program available to a diverse spectrum of consumers. There is a free version of iMovie available for download for iOS devices, and it is a component of the iLife suite, which is pre-installed on all new Macs and may be downloaded for free. Through the use of this strategy, the need for initial expenses is eliminated, enabling users to investigate the capabilities of the program without making any financial commitment. People may need to consider extra fees related to Apple gear, such as Macs, iPads, or iPhones, to fully exploit the features of the program, even though iMovie itself is free. On the other hand, when compared to the majority of professional-grade video editing systems now available on the market, the total cost of ownership is still reasonably affordable. In addition, the integration of Apple's ecosystem guarantees a consistent experience across all devices, which further strengthens the value offer. When choosing software for video editing, it is essential to take into consideration a variety of things in addition to the initial cost. Many factors, including compatibility, ease of use, feature set, and long-term support, are taken into consideration when establishing the overall value proposition. The price model of iMovie, in conjunction with its extensive feature set and seamless integration with Apple's ecosystem, makes it an appealing choice for consumers who are looking for a video editing solution that is both powerful and affordable.

Is iMovie the Right Video Editing Solution for Your Needs?

Raw footage may be transformed into an engaging visual tale with the help of the appropriate video editing software, just like a competent chef can create a culinary masterpiece. iMovie, which is Apple's video editing program that is designed to be user-friendly, provides a comprehensive collection of capabilities that are designed to meet the needs of a diverse range of users, from amateurs to semi-professionals. The capacity of any program to cater to your particular demands and objectives is, however, the most important factor in determining its genuine worth. iMovie allows you to import and organize your video clips, images, and audio files seamlessly, and then you can weave them together using the easy drag-and-drop capability. Anyone with less knowledge in video editing can utilize the program since it has an interface that is straightforward to use. The simple package that is iMovie packs a powerful punch, with functions ranging from the most fundamental, such as cutting and splitting, to the most complex, such as green-screen effects and picture-in-picture overlays. It is essential to have a precise fit, much like a suit that has been expertly fitted. iMovie may not be the best option for pros who are looking for more powerful tools and granular control, even though it shines in terms of its simplicity and convenience of use. The ultimate choice about whether or not to get iMovie has to be based on a comprehensive comprehension of the capabilities of the program as well as the specific requirements that you have.

Benefits of iMovie Editing Application

4K Resolution

iMovie is a movie editing program that supports and exports any film with a quality as high as 4k. This is one of the many reasons why it is so popular among movie industry professionals. Following the addition of any audio overlay or filter to your original film, you will be able to save and export these films once the editing process has been completed. This ability will be available to you. Even when shown on several large displays, it would seem immaculate and seamless.

To give you an example, the majority of movies that are shown in theaters are the traditional high-definition (HD) version, which has a resolution of 1920 by 1080 pixels. In contrast, the 4k video format, which has a resolution of 3840 by 2160 pixels, offers the most immersive movie experience possible.

Beginner-Friendly Interface

Apple recognizes that its iMovie editing software will be used by a wide range of users, not limited to professionals and computer-savvy individuals. This is the reason why the program is constructed in the manner that it is. When compared to the sophisticated picture editing program Photoshop, we have found that iMovie is even simpler to manipulate on the very first step of the design process. You can quickly create a video using iMovie since it offers a variety of themes and templates that you can use to personalize your movie to meet your preferences, preferences, and requirements. The user interface is so straightforward that all of the available options are discernible; all it takes is one week to become proficient with it.

Advanced Editing Features

The editing software included with iMovie is everything from rudimentary and fundamental, although it is so easily accessible and user-friendly. On the other hand, some editing software will just offer you the essentials, such as the ability to add effects or music, but iMovie will supply you with all of these things and much more. iMovie allows you to add effects and improvements to your video, such as voice-overs for documentaries and background music for romantic comedies. Additionally, it will make it possible for you to customize things like trailers that include credit rolls, recommended film templates for a wide variety of film genres and short films, and even the entertaining green-screen effects that may be used for parodies and cartoon-style films.

Complete and Unaltered Original File

A further characteristic that distinguishes the editing software for iMovie from all other editing software is that it does not alter the file that was created. With this tool, you will be able to save the raw and unaltered versions of the stills, videos, and audio that was originally captured for your film. iMovie will save you time and effort by allowing you to keep the original files. This will allow you to avoid the need to create duplicates of each media file before trying to develop your film project. In addition to that, iMovie makes it simple to share content by providing you with the choice to use iCloud or AirDrop. This ensures that you will not lose the fifty hours of effort that you have put into your first film if you accidentally close the program.

Add Voice-Over

Have you ever sat in front of your television and watched David Attenborough narrate everything that was happening on your screen while adorable newborn animals were being adorable? The following is an example of a voice-over, in which a narrator talks in the background as the footage is playing, and you can simply include them in your video using iMovie. Once you have finished recording, choose the **"Plus"** option located on the left side of the interface, and then select **"Voice-Over."** After you have tapped **"Record,"** explain what you want to express, and then click **"Tap"** when you are finished. You can quickly **"Review"** your voice-over, and after you are pleased with it, you can either **"Retake," "Cancel," or "Accept"** the voice-over. Additionally, there is a layer referred to as **"Recording"** that allows you to modify the pace, loudness, and even the length of your recorded recording.

Change Themes

A thematic component is added to the totality of your film production via the use of themes. Selecting the **"Setting"** icon located on the top right side of the screen is all that is required to get started with adding themes. There is a large selection of themes available for you to choose from, including **"Bright," "Playful," "Modern," "Neon," "Travel," "Simple," and "News."** You can choose the theme that you believe best fits the atmosphere you are trying to achieve, and there is also an additional component, such as enhancing a scene with background music that will fade in and out based on your preference. Following the completion of the process of adding themes, you will see that it will be shown on your timeline reel as a green layer that can be simply cut, split, or deleted.

Clip Trimming

In the world of professional film production, trimming clips is often a difficult task; however, the editing program known as iMovie makes this task much simpler for you. For the trimming process, each clip will need to be picked separately. When the yellow highlight appears on either side of the clip, you can quickly and easily drag the edges to your perusal to abbreviate a specific clip through the use of this method. Altering the location of each movie or clip to suit your preferences is another option that may be used in this manner. To do this, you just click and hold the specific trip or sequence, and then move and drag it to conform to the arrangement that you like most.

Filters

The addition of a layer of filter to your video movie is a simple approach to alter the overall atmosphere of the project, and the editing tool iMovie makes it simple to accomplish this transformation. Using the **"Project Settings"** option will provide you with a comprehensive list of video filters that you can use in your film production. One of the most advantageous aspects of this is that you have the option to apply a filter to a single clip, which means that you may personalize each filter for each video clip or still image capture. Choose the clip to which you want to apply a filter, and then pick the "Filter" icon located at the bottom of the interface, and then select the filter you want to apply from the list of options that are shown to you. The following are some of the available filters: **"Comic," "Blue," "Duotone," and "Silent Era,"** amongst a great number of others.

Speed Up and Slow Down

When you use iMovie, you can instantly adjust the speed of your video production to either a faster or slower pace. You can also change the frame rate of each clip, which will allow you to create a movie project that is consistent from the very first scene to the very final scene. To begin, you will need to pick the "**Clock**" button located in the bottom right corner of the timeline of your project. After that, you will need to click on a clip that you wish to change. You may choose whether you want the footage to be played at a slow or fast rate. The custom speeds that are accessible may be readily customized by inputting your unique speed, which is available to you. There is a slider that can be found on the top portion of the interface, and when you make a change to the pace of the clip, a turtle or a rabbit will appear in the center of the clip to indicate that you have successfully made the change. On your timeline, the clip that has been sped up will seem shorter, whilst the clips that have been slowed down will continue to grow longer.

The Split Clip

Depending on what you want to do and how you see the final product, the iMovie editing program allows you to divide a single clip into two or multiple smaller parts. Additionally, you can trim and rearrange clips inside your timeline. You can divide a clip in your iMovie program by clicking on a clip on the timeline that you wish to change and split, and then simply positioning the playhead on the area of the clip where you want to break the picture or video. Once that is complete, go to the "**Modify**" setting and choose the "**Split Clip**" option.

Add Text

You will be able to add a title at the beginning of your film project, captions, or subtitles to make your film accessible to everyone and you will also be able to simply add credits after your movie project if you add text to your film project. In addition to providing you with the ability to simply time the text where you want it to appear in your timeline, the iMovie editing program offers a wide range of font styles that can be customized to adapt to any theme that your movie may have. After you have gone through the process of selecting the font style that is suitable for your movie, you can then input the text, and it will display on the screen in a way that allows you to effortlessly drag it to the location that you want.

Add Audio

The use of background music is an essential component of every movie. At times, it is that special facet of a movie that is responsible for making it unforgettable. Through the use of the iMovie editing program, you can include music in your video production, which will allow you to portray that sensation. To include audio or background music in your movie, pick "**Audio**" from the menu that appears above the program interface. Click on "**Music**," "**Sound Effects** "or" GarageBand" on the sidebar. The list of each selection will display, and you will be able to simply filter it to discover the music or any audio effects that you are looking for. After that, choose the clip to which you wish to add background music or sound effects, and then drag the music below the clip on the timeline of the project. In addition, any audio can be edited to a great extent; all you need to do is click on the "**Trim background music**" option inside the movie settings to implement this feature.

Add Transitions

By including transitions in your movies, you can create a unified project that flows seamlessly, ensuring that each video will continue to mix in with the one that comes after it. For each video clip, you have the option of allowing it to fade out to dissolve into another still image or zoom in to another scene in your movie, depending on what you want to do. This may be done either automatically or manually. It is necessary to go to the "**Transitions**" option located in the top portion of the interface to manually create a transition for each segment. A preview of a transition may also be obtained by just skimming the cursor over the special effect. To include a transition between two stills, you may do this by dragging an effect between the two clips that you have chosen on your timeline. If you want to create a transitional effect at the beginning and conclusion of a clip, you need to double-click the transition that you have selected.

iMovie Editing: Add Subtitles or Captions

Although there is not currently a function in iMovie editing that is specifically designed for captioning and adding subtitles, it is feasible to do so by using the Title option at the moment. The title option is quite flexible; even if it will need some effort, it is possible to change anything from the font color to the location of the caption. Proceed to the filmstrip section as soon as you have finished importing your movie. By clicking on the "**Titles**" option and selecting the "**Lower**" style, you can type a conversation that is five seconds long. It is important to remember to alter the text length so that it fits well. Each of the text blocks will be shown on the filmstrip that is located on the timeline of the project, and you can modify it so that it is in rhythm with the soundtrack of the film. To copy and paste the text throughout the five seconds of the still image, go to the text box and press the **Ctrl+C** and **Ctrl+V** keys simultaneously. Once the text has been altered and centered on the bottom section of the video, copy and paste the text. After you have mastered this method, it will be simple for you to transcribe your movie and add subtitles to it. Have a good time, since adding subtitles is almost always the best course of action!

How to understand iMovie

Getting acquainted with the interface, capabilities, and workflow of iMovie is necessary to get an understanding of the program.

To assist you in getting started, the following is a step-by-step guide:

1. Use the iMovie program on your Mac or iOS device to begin the iMovie launch process.

2. Interface Overview:

- iMovie's user interface is easy to use. When using the Mac version, the toolbar is located at the very top, the viewer is located in the middle, and the timeline is located at the very beginning. The media libraries and project settings are located in the sidebar that is located on the left.
- On iOS devices, the user interface is designed for touch interaction with identical components, but it has been changed for smaller displays.
3. Import Media
- To import media files (videos, images, and music) from your computer or device into the media library, either clicks the "**Import Media**" button or drags and drop the items into the media library.
4. Create a New Project
- To start a new project, you must first click on the "**Create New**" button.
- As part of your project, you will need to choose the aspect ratio and resolution.
- To save your project, you will need to give it a name and choose a location.
5. Add Media to Timeline
- To begin creating your movie, add media clips from the media library to the timeline by dragging and dropping them.
- By dragging clips along the timeline, you can arrange them in the order that you want them to appear.
6. Transitions and Effects
- The visual attractiveness of your video may be improved with the help of a variety of transitions and effects that are available in iMovie.
- To create a transition between clips, using the Transitions browser, drag a transition and drop it between two clips on the timeline. This will add a transition between the clips.
- Choosing a clip in the timeline and selecting it from the Effects browser is the first step in applying effects.
7. Titles and Credits
- By choosing the titles and credits you want to add to your movie from the Titles browser and dragging them into the timeline, you may add them to your video.
8. Export your Movie
- Export your project by selecting "**Share**" from the "**File**" menu when you have completed your movie and are pleased with it.
- Make your selections for the export parameters you want, including the resolution and the file format.
- To save your video, click the "**Next**" button and then choose a location to store it.
9. Share your Movie
- Once the exporting process is complete, you have the option of sending your video to social media networks, sending it via email, or saving it to your device for later viewing.

How to organize your media

It is very necessary to organize your media in iMovie 2024 to provide a seamless editing procedure.

1. The first step is to import your media files into iMovie. Your media files should be imported. Either by dragging and dropping files straight into the iMovie interface or by clicking on the Import button that is located in the toolbar, you can do this. Your video clips, images, and audio files should be imported into the iMovie library on your computer.

2. You can organize your media by creating events, which are containers for the media. You have the option of organizing your material by date, location, or any other criterion that is necessary for your project. Alternatively, you can establish distinct events for each of the projects that you are working on. Go to the File menu, pick "**New Event**," and then give the event a descriptive name. This will allow you to create a new event.

3. The next step is to begin arranging your clips inside each event once you have established your events. Once you have done this, you can begin organizing your clips. Clips may be rearranged, trimmed, or deleted as necessary by dragging and dropping them into the appropriate location. There is also the option to add ratings and keywords to your video, which will make it simpler to locate them in the future.

4. iMovie 2024 may feature smart collections, which automatically categorize your material depending on factors like date, keywords, or ratings. You may use these collections to manage your media. Use these clever groupings to your advantage to locate the clips you want for your project in a short amount of time.

5. During the editing process, adding keywords and ratings to your clips might assist you in locating the video you need more expediently. To add keywords, choose a clip and then click the Info button located in the toolbar. This will allow you to add keywords. You will then be able to add descriptive keywords to your clips, which will assist you in classifying them.

6. Once you have arranged your media in events and smart collections, you can begin the process of constructing your project. Choosing the necessary parameters for your project, such as aspect ratio and resolution, may be accomplished by going to the File menu, selecting "**New Project**," and then selecting the relevant options.

7. You can begin adding clips to your project after you have created it. You can begin adding clips from your events and smart collections to the timeline once you have created your project. When you are creating your final film, you can drag and drop clips from the iMovie collection into the timeline in the order that you want them to appear.

8. As you continue to edit your project, you may need to continue arranging your media to maintain a clean and organized environment. To maintain track of your media while you are working, you may make use of the folders, labels, and other organizing options that are available inside iMovie.

How to get around the interface

The following procedures should be followed to move about the UI in iMovie 2024:

1. Open the iMovie application on your device to begin the process.

2. If you already have projects in progress, you will be able to see them in the list. By clicking on the "**Create New**" option, you can either choose the project that you wish to work on or begin a new version of the project.

3. Main Interface

- **Toolbar**: The toolbar is located at the very top of the user interface. It consists of several buttons that are used for a variety of activities, including the importation of media, the addition of titles, and the exportation of your project.
- **Media Library**: In the top left corner of the screen is where you will find the Media Library. This is the location where you will import your media assets (videos, photographs, and music) to use in your project.
- **Viewer**: This is the viewer, which can be found in the upper-right corner of the interface. At this point, you will be able to preview your project and make further modifications.
- **Timeline**: Within the UI, the timeline can be seen at the very bottom of the screen. It is in this section that you will organize your media clips, create transitions, and make modifications to your whole project.

4. Import Media

- In the toolbar, choose the "**Import Media**" button and start the process.
- To import media files from your computer or other connected devices, you must first choose the files you want to import.

5. **Editing**

- If you want to add media clips to your project, you can do so by dragging them from the media library into the timeline.
- The clips can be trimmed and divided by clicking on them in the timeline and then using the editing tools that show after the click.
- To add transitions between clips, click on the "**Transitions**" tab in the toolbar and then drag a transition between two clips in the timeline. This will add a transition between the clips.

- Adding titles, effects, and audio may be accomplished by clicking on the tabs in the toolbar that correspond to these elements and then dragging them to the timeline.
6. Preview and Playback
- To play, stop, rewind, and fast forward your project, you can make use of the playback controls that are positioned above the viewer.
- You can see your project from a certain point in time by clicking on the playhead that is located on the timeline.
7. Export
- Once you have completed the editing of your project, you should choose the "**Share**" option located in the toolbar.
- Make your selections for the export options that you want, including the resolution, quality, and file type.
- To export your project, you will need to "**Next**" click the button.

It is important to remember to save your project regularly by using the keyboard shortcut (Command + S) or by choosing "**Save**" from the "**File**" menu.

iMovie customization options

iMovie has a wide variety of modification tools that can be used to improve your films, including the following:

1. **Themes**: iMovie offers a wide variety of pre-designed themes that include titles, transitions, and music selections that are compatible with each other. It is possible to choose a theme that corresponds with the atmosphere or style of your video.
2. **Titles**: You can add titles to your films to categorize portions, offer context, or introduce additional sequences. For your personalization, iMovie provides a variety of title designs, fonts, and animations to choose from.
3. **Transitions**: Select from a wide range of transitions to provide a seamless transition from one clip to the next. You can modify the length of transitions as well as their style to accommodate the pace of your film.
4. **Filters**: To improve the overall visual appeal of your movie, iMovie comes equipped with several filters and effects out of the box. You can create the desired appearance by adjusting the strength of the filters.
5. **Soundtracks**: iMovie has a collection of royalty-free soundtracks and sound effects that you can use to enhance your films. You may use them to make your videos more interesting. Moreover, you can import your own audio and music files.
6. **Split screen**: To show several films or photos at the same time, you may create split-screen effects and use them. iMovie allows you to personalize the layout as well as the size of each screen.
7. **Speed controls**: You can create fast-motion or slow-motion effects by adjusting the speed of your video clips using the speed controls. In addition, you may reverse clips to create one-of-a-kind visual effects.

8. **Color Correction**: Make adjustments to the brightness, contrast, saturation, and white balance of your film by using the color correction tools that are available in iMovie. Additionally, you can apply color presets to make alterations quickly.
9. **Green screen:** One of the effects that iMovie provides is called green screen, which is sometimes known as chroma key. This effect enables you to change the backdrop of a clip with another picture or video.
10. **Advanced Editing Tools:** iMovie provides you with sophisticated editing capabilities, such as picture-in-picture effects, audio tweaks, and precise cutting, which give you greater control over your film.
11. **Sharing Options:** Once you have finished customizing your movie, you can simply share it straight to social media networks, export it to a variety of file formats, or even burn it using a DVD burner.

CHAPTER TWO
SETTING UP

Overview

Chapter two talks about setting up iMovie 2024 on your device. Additionally, it also discusses how you can create a new project, and import your existing project.

How to set up iMovie

Whenever you launch iMovie for the first time, it will open in the Projects view. To begin working on a movie project, choose **Create New** and then select **Movie** from the menu that appears.

Following the beginning of a new movie project, you will be able to take use of the Libraries list located in the sidebar to access your picture library and import both video and still images.

To access your media without having to create a new project, you can do so by clicking the Media button that is located on the toolbar.

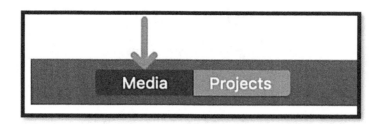

Add media from your photo library in iMovie on Mac

The iMovie application can automatically access and use all of the photographs and video clips that are stored in your Photos, iPhoto, and Aperture libraries. Take note that versions of the Mac operating system that are later than macOS Mojave 10.14 do not support the usage of Aperture or iPhoto. If your photographs are stored in an Aperture or iPhoto library, you can convert your portfolio to Photos.

Here are the steps:

1. The first step is to choose your picture library from the list of libraries that appear in the iMovie software on your Mac.
2. Select a content category by clicking the pop-up menu at the top of the browser, and then navigate through the thumbnails of the photographs and video clips that fall under that category.
3. To get a preview of the picture or video clip that you want to utilize, choose it in the viewer.
4. **Choose from the following options:**
   - To insert the picture or video clip, drag it to the timeline between clips or between a clip and a transition. This will allow you to insert it seamlessly.
   - While you are dragging, a blue box will emerge in the timeline. This box will indicate the location in the timeline where the picture or clip will be shown.
   - You can replace a clip by dragging the picture or clip into the timeline and placing it on top of the clip.

A white border will emerge around the clip in the timeline as you bring it closer to the timeline. Immediately after you let go of the mouse button, choose **Replace** from the menu that displays. In the timeline, the picture or clip takes the place of the shorter clip.

Create a new movie project in iMovie on Mac

To make a movie, you must first make a movie project of your own. While you are working on a video project, iMovie will save automatically; you do not need to save as you go. This is an important feature.

1. To begin, open the Projects window inside the iMovie application on your Mac.

2. After clicking the **Create New button**, choose **Movie**.

3. Click the **Projects back button** located on the left side of the toolbar (as seen below), and then click the **Create New button**. This will allow you to do so while you are editing a project.

If you have more than one iMovie library open, choose the library where you want the video to be stored by clicking the pop-up menu labeled "**Library**." Once your project has been created, you may add clips to it by selecting events from the Libraries list and browsing through your Photos collection. If you return to the Projects view, you will be prompted to provide a name for the project. It is the initial clip that you upload to the timeline that will establish the resolution and frame rate of the movie project that you are working on. For 1080p and 720p video, iMovie now supports frame rates greater than 30 frames per second (fps), and it now supports 4K video at 30 frames per second (fps). If you want the resolution of your project to be adjusted to 4K, the first clip that you upload to the timeline must be a 4K clip. The first 1080p or 720p clip that you upload to the timeline must be a 60 fps clip if you want your project to be set at 60 frames per second from the beginning.

How to import your media files

You can choose to import video clips and still photographs that you have taken with your iPad, iPhone, or iPod touch.

The steps:

1. Make sure that your device is turned on and then connect it to your Mac by using the USB cord that was included with the device.
2. After opening the iMovie program on your Mac, access the Import window by clicking the Import button that is located in the instrument bar.

To import files, first click the **Media button** in the toolbar, and then click the Import button. If you do not see the Import button, click the **Media button**.

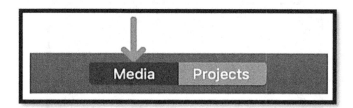

Immediately shut the window if the Image Capture, Photos, or any other photo application opens.

3. Under the Import box, go to the Cameras part of the sidebar and choose your device under that area. The thumbnails of the video clips and photographs that are stored on your device are shown in the Import box.
4. To preview a video, either slide the cursor left and right over a video thumbnail or place the pointer over the preview at the top of the Import window and click the **Play button** ▶. Both of these options are available throughout the preview process.

Clicking the **Previous or Next button** will take you to the previous or next clip, respectively. Alternatively, you can click and hold the Previous or Next button to rewind or fast-forward through the video.

5. **Take one of the following actions to designate the location where the imported media will be stored:**

- **Choose an existing event:** The event may be selected by clicking the "**Import** to" pop-up option that is located at the very top of the Import window.

- **Create a new event:** This will allow you to create a new event by selecting New Event from the "**Import** to" pop-up menu, typing in a name for the new event, and then clicking the OK button.

6. **Choose one of the following options:**

- **Import every clip:** Click the Import All button.
- **Import selected clips:** Perform a command-click on each clip that you want to import, and then click the Import Selected button (the name of the Import button will change).

Following the closing of the Import window, your clips will be shown in the event. A progress indicator may appear in the upper-right corner of the window while the clips are being imported. This visibility will be contingent on the length of each clip as well as the number of clips that you are importing.

As the import process is being completed, you are free to continue working in iMovie.

7. Once your media has been imported, you should unplug the device.

Import into iMovie on Mac from file-based cameras

The ability to capture and save video clips and photographs on flash-based storage or hard disk drives (HDD) is a feature that is available in file-based cameras and devices. Typically, a USB cable is used to establish a connection between your computer and file-based cameras and gadgets. Certain file-based cameras come with detachable memory cards that may be inserted into your Mac instead of the camera itself.

1. **Choose from the following options:**
- Make sure that your device is turned on and then connect it to your Mac by using the cord that was included with the device.

You should switch the camcorder to the PC Connect mode if you are using it. There is a possibility that the name of this transfer option will be different on your device. After you have connected your camcorder to your Mac, it may immediately enter the "connect" mode. The documentation that was included with your equipment might provide you with further information. Take note that if you connect a DVD camcorder to your Mac, the DVD Player application can immediately launch. Should this occur, you should just exit the DVD Player.

- If your device makes use of an SD card, you will need to remove the card from the device and then place it either into the card slot on your Mac (if your Mac has a card slot) or into an external card reader.

You can launch the Import window in the iMovie software on your Mac by clicking the Import button that is located in the toolbar. To import files, first click the **Media button** in the toolbar, and then click the **Import button**. If you do not see the Import button, click the **Media button**.

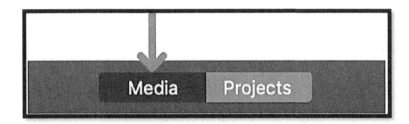

Immediately shut the window if the Image Capture, Photos, or any other photo application opens.

2. Once you are in the Import box, go to the Cameras area of the sidebar and choose your device.

The thumbnails of the video clips and photographs that are stored on your device are shown in the Import box. The Import window will provide a preview of the item that you have selected at the very top of the window. Take note that to display just photos or only videos, you must choose an option from the pop-up menu that appears in the upper-right corner of the Import window.

3. If you want to preview a video, you may either drag the cursor left and right over a video thumbnail or move the pointer over the preview that is located at the top of the Import window and then click the **Play button** ▶ .

Clicking the **Previous or Next button** will take you to the previous or next clip, respectively. Alternatively, you can click and hold the Previous or Next button to rewind or fast-forward through the video.

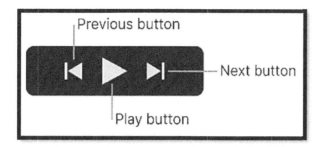

Previous button

Next button

Play button

4. One of the following must be done to designate the location where the imported media will be stored:

- **Choose an existing event**: The event may be selected by clicking the "**Import to**" pop-up option that is located at the very top of the Import window.

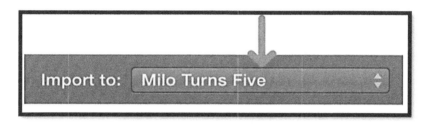

Import to: Milo Turns Five

- To create a new event, choose **New Event** from the pop-up menu that appears at the top of the Import window, and then click OK. After that, input a name for the new event and click the "**Import to**" button.

Take one of the following actions:

- **Import all clips**: Click the **Import All button**.
- **Import selected clips**: Perform a command-click on each clip that you want to import, and then click the **Import Selected button** (the name of the Import button will change).

Following the closing of the Import window, your clips will be shown in the event. A progress indicator may appear in the upper-right corner of the window while the clips are being imported. This visibility will be contingent on the length of each clip as well as the number of clips that you are importing. As the import process is being completed, you are free to continue working in iMovie.

5. As soon as your media has been imported, you should unplug the device.

Import into iMovie on Mac from tape-based cameras

It is possible to play the video that you have imported from tape-based cameras by utilizing the controls that are included in the Import box. This allows you to choose which clips to import.

Direct video (including DVCAM and DVCPRO) and high-definition video (HDV) are the formats that can be imported from tape.

1. Use the cord that was included with the tape-based camera to establish a connection between your Mac and the camera.

You may make adjustments to the settings on your camera for iMovie to be able to manage it. If your Mac does not have a FireWire port but does have a Thunderbolt port, you may connect the FireWire connection by using either an Apple Thunderbolt to FireWire Adapter or an Apple Thunderbolt Display (which also has a FireWire port). Both of these options are described in more detail below. It is advised that you import the video using the same camera that you used to capture it to get the best possible results when importing from a camera that requires the usage of tape.

2. Activate the camera and choose either the VTR or VCR mode from the menu.

Your camera may use a different moniker for this setting. To get further details, please refer to the paperwork that was included with your camera.

3. In the iMovie application on your Mac, open the **Import window** by clicking the **Import button** located in the toolbar.

To import files, first click the **Media button** in the toolbar, and then click the **Import button**. If you do not see the Import button, click the **Media button**.

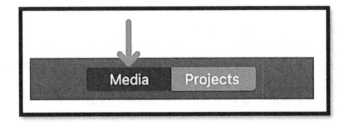

Immediately shut the window if the Image Capture, Photos, or any other photo application opens.

4. In the Import window, go to the Cameras section of the sidebar and pick the tape-based camera that you want to import. When you open the Import window, the picture that is now being shown on the tape will be displayed.

5. To preview the video, you must first drag the cursor over the preview that is located at the top of the Import window and then click the **Play button** .

Clicking the Previous or Next button will take you to the previous or next clip, respectively. Alternatively, you may click and hold the Previous or Next button to rewind or fast-forward through the video.

6. Take one of the following actions to define the location where the imported media will be stored:

- **Choose an existing event:** The event may be selected by clicking the "**Import to**" pop-up option that is located at the very top of the Import window.
- **Create a new event:** To create a new event, choose **New Event** from the pop-up menu that appears at the top of the Import window, then click OK. After that, input a name for the new event and click the "**Import to**" button.

7. Simply click the **Import button** after you have located the place on the tape where you wish to start the import process. Video is imported from cassettes into iMovie in real-time, which means that the time it takes to import the video is the same amount of time it takes to see it play.

8. Click the **Stop Import button** after the portion of the video that you wish to import has been imported. IMovie can continue importing until it reaches the end of the tape if you do not click the Stop Import button. Click the Import button after you have used the playback controls to move your tape to a different place where you wish to start importing the video. This will allow you to import another segment of the film.

9. Once you have finished importing, you may dismiss the Import window by clicking the dismiss button.

Several media formats in iMovie

Apple's video editing program, iMovie, is compatible with a wide range of media formats, allowing users to import and edit any of them.

These are some of the most common formats that it can support:

1. The following video formats are supported: MP4, MOV, M4V, and AVI (provided that the relevant codec is present).
2. Common audio formats are MP3, WAV, AIFF, and AAC.
3. The following are the image formats: JPEG, PNG, TIFF, and GIF
4. **Cameras and Camcorder Formats:** A great number of digital cameras and camcorders output films in formats such as AVCHD and MPEG-2, which iMovie can import and work with.
5. **Apple ProRes:** iMovie is compatible with the Apple ProRes format, which is a high-quality video compression format designed by Apple. iMovie also supports the Apple ProRes format.
6. **HEVC (H.265) protocol:** IMovie also can import and work with movies that have been encoded using the High-Efficiency Video Coding (HEVC) standard, which is also referred to as H.265.

CHAPTER THREE
EDITING TECHNIQUES

Overview

In this chapter, you will learn all there is to know about several editing techniques in iMovie 2024 including trimming videos, cutting videos, using a precision editor, and speeding and slowing down videos in iMovie

How to trim video in iMovie

Adjusting the duration of a clip in your movie is possible by manipulating the clip's start or end point, or by modifying the duration of a selected range. Adjusting the start and end points and modifying clip durations is known as trimming.

Drag the clip in the timeline to either extend or shorten its duration

The steps:

1. In the iMovie app on your Mac, you can easily skim to the beginning or end of a clip in the timeline that you want to extend or shorten.
2. **Choose one of the following options:**
   - Drag the edge of the clip away from its center to extend it. To extend a clip, it is necessary to have unused portions of the clip at your disposal.
   - Drag the edge of the clip towards its center to shorten it.

Add or remove frames with the clip trimmer

The clip trimmer allows you to add or remove frames from a clip, giving you more control over its content. It is also possible to track the amount of your clip that is being used.

1. To trim a clip in the timeline of the iMovie app on your Mac, simply select the desired clip.
2. To access the Clip Trimmer, go to the **Window menu** and select **Show Clip Trimmer**. A clip trimmer is displayed above the timeline.

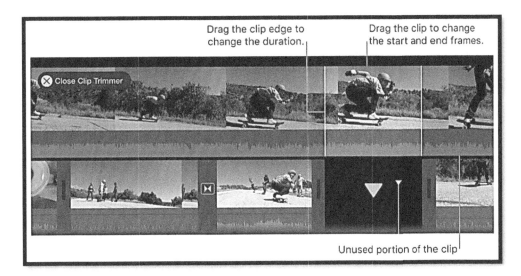

3. **Choose one of the following options:**
   - To extend the clip, simply drag the edge of the clip away from its center.
   - Drag the edge of the clip towards its center to shorten it.
   - Ensure that the clip maintains its original length, but adjust the start and end frames by dragging the clip from its center and moving it left or right.
4. Press the **Return key** to close the clip trimmer.

Refine the start and end points and craft split edits using the precision editor

The precision editor allows you to make precise adjustments to the timing of your clips and the duration of transitions between them. The precision editor allows you to extend the audio in a clip beyond the boundaries of the video. This is useful when you want the audio from one clip to continue during the next clip, or when you want the audio from a clip to start before the video. Split edits refer to edits where the audio and video of a clip have different start or end points.

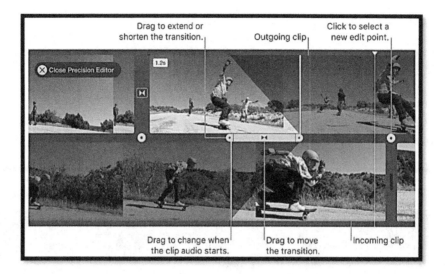

Drag to extend or shorten the transition.   Outgoing clip   Click to select a new edit point.

1.2s

Close Precision Editor

Drag to change when the clip audio starts.   Drag to move the transition.   Incoming clip

1. **Within the iMovie app on your Mac, follow these steps:**
- Click twice on the edge of a clip in the timeline.
- To access the Precision Editor, simply click on the edge of a clip in the timeline and then go to **Window > Show Precision Editor**.

The precision editor is displayed, providing a more detailed perspective of your outgoing and incoming clips. In the precision editor, a gray vertical line is used to represent the edit point, which is where the outgoing clip is replaced by the incoming clip. The clip that is currently playing and the clips that come before it is displayed at the top of the precision editor, while the clip that is about to play and the clips that come after it are displayed below. The faded sections on either side of the edit line represent the unused parts of the clips that can be trimmed. These areas can be skimmed to assist in determining where to make cuts. When a transition is attached to the selected edit point, you can easily identify its duration by looking for diagonal lines and a transition bar with handles.

2. Drag the edit line in the center of the precision editor or adjust the duration of the clips by dragging them.
3. To make changes to a transition, you can follow one of these steps:
- To make the transition shorter, you can either drag the incoming transition handle to the right or drag the outgoing transition handle to the left.
- Extend the duration of the transition by adjusting the position of the transition handles.
4. To adjust the audio edit point, simply position the pointer over the blue waveform of the outgoing or incoming clip, and effortlessly drag the audio edit point to the desired location.

Note that to move an audio edit point, it is necessary to enable the Show Waveforms option in the timeline. To ensure that your video and audio clips are displayed with audio waveforms, you can follow these steps: Click on Settings located in the upper-right corner of the timeline, and then simply select the Show Waveforms checkbox.

5. After you've completed moving the clips, edit points, or transition handles, simply press **Return** to close the precision editor. To choose a different edit point in the precision editor, simply click on one of the dots located on the border between the incoming and outgoing clips.

Trim unwanted frames using the shortcut menu

1. To select the range of frames you want to keep in the iMovie app on your Mac, simply press and hold the R key and drag across a clip in the timeline.
2. To trim the selection, simply control-click the clip and select "**Trim Selection**" from the shortcut menu.

The clip is cut to fit within the selected boundaries.

How to Move and Split Clips in iMovie on Mac

The clips in the timeline can be rearranged and divided into separate parts.

Move clips in the timeline

- To move clips in the timeline, simply select one or more clips in the iMovie app on your Mac and drag them to a new location.

- The timeline displays blue outlines to indicate the placement of the clips.

Split a clip

1. To split a clip in the timeline of the iMovie app on your Mac, simply select the desired clip.
2. Place the playhead at the desired location to divide the clip.
3. Select **Modify > Split Clip**.

How to cut videos in iMovie on Mac

Important information you need to know

- To trim a clip in iMovie on a desktop or mobile, simply select the clip and drag it in from either edge.
- Click the desired position in iMovie on a Mac, then press **Command-B** to split the clip.
- On an iPhone or iPad, you can easily split a video by following these steps: long-tap the video roll, drag your finger to the desired position, tap "**Actions**," and then tap "**Split**."
- After splitting the video into separate clips, you have the option to remove any unwanted parts.

iMovie is a highly popular video editing app among Apple device users, such as Mac and iPhone users, when it comes to cutting videos. iMovie is a highly versatile video editing program that offers a wide range of functions, including video trimming, adding transitions, and incorporating subtitles, among others. In addition, this application is widely used by professional editors for video editing purposes. Unfortunately, some users struggle with utilizing iMovie's video trimming function.

Here's a guide on how to split videos in iMovie on your Mac:

1. First, you need to access the app. If iMovie is not already downloaded on your Mac device, you will need to download the app and install it. After the installation is complete, simply open iMovie on your device.

2. Import your video. Clicking on the **Create New option** on the app's first interface will bring up two options: Movie and Trailer. Choose the **Movie option** to trim your video. To import your video, simply click on the Import icon located on the left side of the interface.

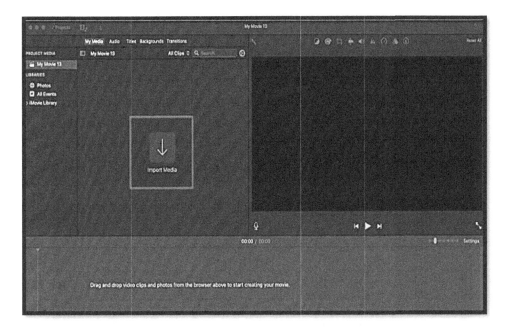

3. Drag the video to the Timeline. Once you've uploaded your video, simply hold and drag the video file to the Timeline. The Timeline can be found below the interface.

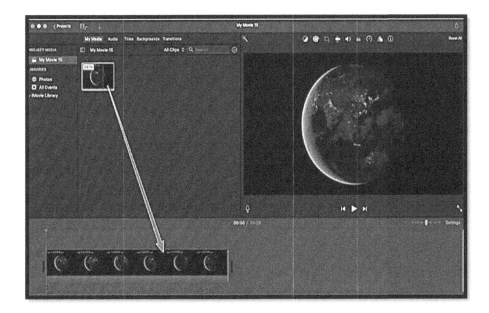

4. Trim the video. To trim your video, choose the video on your Timeline. Next, position the cursor at the start or end of your video to activate the trimming arrows. Next, adjust the starting and ending points of your video to trim it.
5. Exporting your video To save the selected part of your video, simply click on the Export icon located at the top right of the interface. Next, choose the **Export File button** from the pop-up menu. After that, proceed by clicking the **Next button**. Name your file and click Save on the next interface.

Different splitting techniques in iMovie 2024

When using iMovie 2024, you have access to a range of splitting techniques that can greatly enhance your video editing experience.

Here are a few commonly used methods:

1. **Standard Split:** This technique is commonly used for splitting. Position the playhead at the desired point in the video to split the clip. Next, simply click on the clip to select it. To split the clip at the playhead position, simply press Command+B (Mac) or Ctrl+B (Windows).
2. **Blade Tool**: The Blade Tool enables you to precisely cut a clip at any desired point. To split the clip at the desired point, simply select the blade tool from the toolbar and click on the clip. This method is highly effective for precise editing.
3. **Precision Editor**: The precision editor in iMovie enables you to make precise adjustments to split points. To open the precision editor, simply double-click on a clip. Split points can

be easily adjusted by dragging them left or right, allowing for smooth transitions between clips.

4. **Splitting Audio and Video**: Occasionally, there may be a need to separate the audio and video components of a clip individually. To accomplish this, you can select the clip and then choose "Detach Audio" from the Modify menu. It is possible to separate the audio and video tracks individually.

5. **Splitting Clips in the Timeline**: Clips can be split in the timeline as well, in addition to being split in the viewer. To split the clip, just place the playhead at the desired position and press Command+B (Mac) or Ctrl+B (Windows) while the clip is selected.

6. **Splitting Clips During Playback**: During playback, if you wish to divide a clip at a particular point, you can use the "**Split Clip at Playhead**" command. To split the clip at the current playhead position, press Command+Shift+S (Mac) or Ctrl+Shift+S (Windows) while the video is playing.

How to use the precision editor

The Precision Editor, much like the Clip Trimmer, is not considered a crucial tool for mastering iMovie and creating movies. If you've ever had difficulty achieving the desired transition between two clips, the Precision Editor is worth exploring. The Clip Trimmer allows you to easily determine the starting and ending points of a clip, while the Precision editor allows you to carefully consider how a Transition effect will impact the transition between clips. This can be incredibly useful for addressing issues in your edits, like seamlessly removing any unwanted video fragments as you transition out of a clip. The Precision Editor is designed to enhance your transition between clips. To access it, you can either double-click on the edge of a clip or select an edge of a clip and choose Show Precision Editor from the Window menu. Below is a screenshot with two clips that have been trimmed and positioned as desired, separated by a Transition effect (indicated by the green arrow).

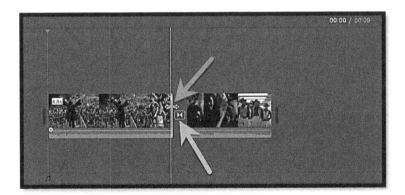

Observe that the pointer (indicated by the red arrow) has transformed from its typical arrow symbol to two arrows pointing sideways. We are positioned at the edge of the clip, allowing me to easily open the Precision Editor with a double-click.

Upon opening the Precision Editor, the appearance of my timeline has been altered:

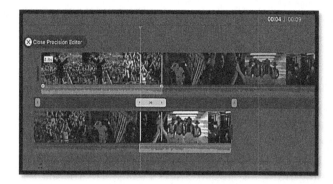

Although it may appear complex, the Precision Editor provides valuable information to assist you in achieving a more accurate edit. For some reason, the outgoing clip has been placed on top of the incoming clip. This is different from the previous screenshot where the transition was on the left side. The Precision Editor aims to display the entire untrimmed footage in both clips, allowing us to make precise adjustments to our transition. In addition, you can adjust the duration of the transition effect by clicking on either of the black dots located at the edges of the grey box. The right dot is conveniently close to where the red arrow is pointing. The Precision editor provides a clear visual representation of how your clip will appear when played back, allowing you to easily adjust the transition's position and duration.

How to Adjust Your Audio Transitions

The audio in clips transitions in iMovie along the same diagonal line as the video. As a result, the outgoing clip's audio fades out while the incoming clip's audio fades in. It is important to note that regardless of the type or duration of the Transition you choose, the audio in both clips will automatically adjust to match the video. However, there are two ways to modify this in the Precision Editor. You can adjust the start and end points of the audio separately from the video. Below is a screenshot with a red arrow indicating a vertical blue bar. By clicking and dragging, you can adjust the starting point for the audio playback of the clip.

This feature is useful when you need the audio of the incoming clip to begin before the Transition itself starts. It's a surprisingly common occurrence - there's often a certain satisfaction in anticipating what comes next. Another method for adjusting the audio transition is by using the audio fade handles. The screenshot above shows a small semi-circle of light blue, indicated by the green arrow. This is the audio fade handle. Dragging a fade handle toward the center of the clip will cause another diagonal line to appear over the audio. This line indicates how the audio will fade in (or fade out if you are dragging the audio handle from the end of the clip in). By fine-tuning the timing of each clip's audio start and stop, as well as adjusting the fade handles for both the outgoing and incoming clips, you have full control over the audio transition to achieve your desired outcome.

How to speed up and slow down video

Would you like to create a YouTube video that stands out from the rest? Maybe you've created a hilarious home video where you've pulled a prank on someone close to you. Or you're creating a brief instructional video for work that falls slightly short of the desired duration. If you find yourself in such situations, you might consider adjusting the speed of your videos using a video editor. Fortunately, iMovie on your Mac simplifies the process of creating fast and slow-motion videos. To follow the guide, open iMovie on your Mac or download it from the App Store if it's not already installed. If you're new to video editing, it might be helpful to check out our tips for editing videos on a Mac before you get started. Now, let's begin with preparing your clip.

1. **First, you'll need to get the video clip ready**

Begin by adding the video to your timeline. When you open iMovie, start by creating a new project and then import the video. After completing the task, simply move the video to the timeline to begin the editing process. To proceed, you'll need to segment the specific part of the clip you want to adjust the speed of. For this task, carefully review or play through the clip, and pause at the desired starting point for adding the effect. To split the clip, you can either press Command-B or navigate to **Modify > Split Clip** in the menu bar. This will generate the initial version.

Afterward, locate the specific moment on the timeline where you desire the video to resume its regular speed. Follow the same method to cut. A separate clip will be created within the timeline. Now you're all set to apply the effect.

2. **Next, you'll want to apply the effect to the video clip**

There are two methods to adjust the clip's speed. It is possible to make adjustments using either the designated speed tab or a slider. In the top-right window (viewer), you'll find a variety of tools, including the Speed button that resembles a speedometer. There are four options available: slow, fast, freeze-frame, and custom.

The custom percentage option is particularly handy when you need to adjust the speed by a more precise amount, whether it's to decrease or increase it. Keep in mind that speeds below 100% are slower, while anything above 100% is faster. One intriguing method to adjust the speed is through a slider located directly on the clip. There might be a small gray circle with a black center in the top right corner of the selected clip. If you don't, simply choose the clip you want to modify and then press Command-R. To access the Speed Editor, simply right-click on the clip you have selected and select the option to Show Speed Editor from the context menu.

3. **Personalize and Fine-tune the Video Clip**

If you feel that you have applied an excessive number of effects or are dissatisfied with the outcome, resetting the clip is a straightforward process. To reset the viewer (preview) window, just click on the Reset option located at the far right. This action will remove any speed adjustments made to a clip, giving you a fresh start. It's important to be aware that the clip size will also change on the timeline, so it's crucial to consider the impact on surrounding audio and video clips. It is important to keep in mind that if you have already separated the audio, you will need to make the same adjustments to ensure it matches the clip. It's important to keep in mind that adjusting the speed of an audio clip will affect its pitch as well. The variation in pitch can result in voices sounding either high-pitched and squeaky or low-pitched and monster-like.

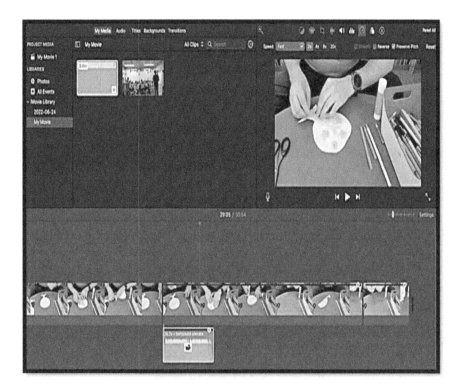

Luckily, iMovie has a convenient feature that preserves the clip's pitch. Located beside the Reset button in the viewer, there is an option called Preserve Pitch. By leaving this option checked, the pitch of the audio clip will remain unchanged, just like in the original file. Once you have finished making all the necessary adjustments, it is important to save your iMovie project and export the edited video.

CHAPTER FOUR
ORGANIZING MEDIA AND EVENTS

Overview

In this chapter, you will learn how to organize your media and events in iMovie 2024. Here, you will see how to create and rename events, duplicate events, merge events and so much more.

Organize Media

When you import video footage into your library, iMovie conveniently organizes the clips into events according to the date and time they were recorded. Events serve as containers for your video clips. Events can be used to group clips in any way you prefer, regardless of their initial time-based grouping. Once an event is chosen from the Libraries list, the clips it contains will be displayed in the browser. To display the Libraries list, simply click on the **Libraries List button** located at the top of the browser.

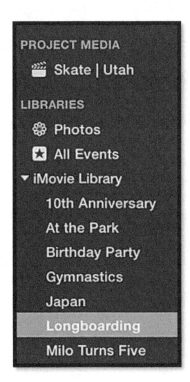

Sort events in the Libraries list

Customize the Libraries list to display events in the order of your preference.

Within the iMovie app on your Mac, you have the option to:

- **Sort events by name:** Click on **View**, then select **Sort Events By**, and choose **Name**.
- **Sort events from newest to oldest:** To sort events from newest to oldest, select **View**, then go to **Sort Events By**. Events in each library are grouped by year when you sort them by date.

How to Create and Rename Events

Here are the steps:

1. Choose the library in the Libraries list on your Mac's iMovie app to create an event.
2. Select **File** and then click on **New Event**. The new event is displayed in the Libraries list, with its name highlighted.
3. Enter a new name to rename the event.

To rename an event that already exists; you can simply select it from the Libraries list, press **Return**, and enter the new name.

Copy or move clips between events

The steps:

1. Open the iMovie app on your Mac and choose an event from the Libraries list that contains the clips you want to move or copy.
2. Choose the clips you want to move or copy in the browser. Remember, if you want to select multiple clips, simply hold down the **Command key** while clicking on the clips you want or drag a selection rectangle around them.
3. Choose one of the following options:
- **Transfer clips between events**: Move the chosen clips from one event to the other.

- **Transfer clips between events:** To move the selected clips from one event to the other, begin by dragging them and then hold down the Option key while dragging.

When you have your project selected below Project Media in the sidebar, dragging clips from the browser will automatically copy them to the destination event.

Duplicate clips

Feel free to make a copy of a clip to experiment with different effects or modifications, all while keeping the original version intact.

1. Open the iMovie app on your Mac and choose the event from the Libraries list that contains the clip you wish to duplicate.
2. Double-click the clip you would like to duplicate. When a portion of a clip is chosen, the entire clip will be duplicated. Remember, if you want to select multiple clips, simply hold down the Command key while clicking on the clips you want, or you can also drag a selection rectangle around the clips.
3. Select **Edit** and then choose **Duplicate Movie**.

Merge or split events

If the footage in the Libraries list is closely related, you have the option to merge (combine) two or more events. It is also possible to divide a single event into multiple events.

Perform the following actions in the iMovie app on your Mac:

- **Merge events:** To merge events, you can either drag an event from the Libraries list to the desired event or select multiple events and choose **File > Merge Events**.

- **Split a single event:** Generate the necessary new events and transfer clips from the original event to the new events.

Delete clips and events

Unwanted clips can be easily removed from an event, and if needed, you have the option to delete the entire event to free up storage space. Note that to free up storage space, it is necessary to delete an entire event. Removing clips from an event does not create additional storage capacity.

1. Open the iMovie app on your Mac and follow these steps:
- **Delete an event:** To delete an event, simply choose the event you want to remove from the Libraries list.
- **Delete clips in an event**: Choose an event from the Libraries list that includes the clips you wish to remove. Then, in the browser, select the specific clips you want to delete.

Remember, if you want to select multiple clips in the same library, simply hold down the **Command key** while clicking on the clips you want to select. Alternatively, you can also drag a selection rectangle around the clips.

2. Select the "**Move to Trash**" option under the **File** menu.

When attempting to delete a clip that is currently being used in a project, a prompt will appear requesting that you first remove the clip from the project before proceeding with the deletion. When you choose a clip and press **Delete**, it will be marked as rejected.

Learn how to efficiently work with multiple libraries in iMovie on your Mac

Your clips are organized into events in the library, along with the projects you create. This guide will explain how to create additional iMovie libraries for various purposes. These libraries can be used to back up your current project, create archives of events and projects on separate storage devices, free up storage space on your Mac by moving iMovie events, and even edit projects on another Mac. It is possible to create additional library files in various locations on your Mac or on different storage devices.

Create a new library

The steps:

1. To open a new library in the iMovie app on your Mac, simply go to **File > Open Library > New**.
2. When the Save dialog pops up, simply enter a name for the new library and choose the desired location to save it. The Movies folder in your home folder is where the default location is set.
3. Click the **Save button**. A new library has been established in the location of your choice, along with an empty event that is set for today's date.

Copy or move clips between libraries or storage devices

The steps:

1. Attach a storage device containing the target library to your Mac, or transfer the target library to your Mac.
2. To access the iMovie app on your Mac, simply navigate to **File > Open Library** and select an option from the submenu. There are several options available to you when it comes to managing your libraries. You can select from libraries that have been recently opened, find a library that already exists on your Mac, or even create a new library. The library you chose is now open in the Libraries list. The first event is selected and its contents are displayed in the browser.
3. Choose the event from the Libraries list that contains the clips you want to move or copy.
4. Choose the clips you want to move or copy in the browser. Remember, if you want to select multiple clips in the same library, simply hold down the Command key while clicking on the clips you want to select. Alternatively, you can also drag a selection rectangle around the clips.
5. **Choose one of the following options:**
- **Move clips between events or libraries**: Move the clip or clips to another event or library.
- **Copy clips between events or libraries:** To move the clip or clips to another event or library, simply start dragging and then hold down the Option key as you drag.

Copy or move events between libraries or storage devices

The steps:

1. Attach a storage device containing the target library to your Mac, or transfer the target library to your Mac.
2. To access your iMovie library on your Mac, simply go to the iMovie app and select **File > Open Library**. From there, you can choose the option that suits your needs from the submenu. There are several options available to you when it comes to managing your libraries. You can select from libraries that have been recently opened, find a library that already exists on your Mac, or even create a new library.

The library you chose is now open in the Libraries list. The first event is selected and its contents are displayed in the browser.

3. Choose the event you wish to move or copy from the Libraries list.
4. **Choose one of the following options:**
- **Move events between libraries**: Move the event to a different library.
- **Copy events between libraries:** To move the event to another library, simply start dragging it and then hold down the **Option key** while dragging.

Copy or move projects between libraries

Follow the steps below:

1. Attach a storage device containing the target library to your Mac, or transfer the target library to your Mac.
2. To access your iMovie library on your Mac, simply go to the iMovie app and select File > Open Library. From there, you can choose the option that suits your needs. There are several options available to you when it comes to managing your libraries. You can select from libraries that have been recently opened, find a library that already exists on your Mac, or even create a brand-new library.

The selected library is displayed in the Libraries list, with the initial event highlighted and its contents shown in the browser.

3. Click on the **Projects button** located in the toolbar.

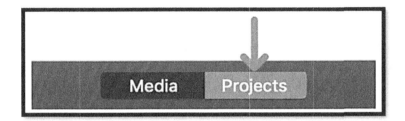

4. Choose the project you wish to move or copy.
5. Click the button located on the right side of the project name, and then choose one of the following options:

- To copy the project to another library, simply follow these steps: Click on "**Copy to Library**" and select the desired library from the submenu.
- To move the project to another library, simply click on "**Move to Library**" and select the desired library from the submenu.

Converting incompatible media in iMovie on Mac

The inclusion of support for video formats that rely on QuickTime 7 in macOS Mojave 10.14 marks the end of an era, as Apple makes the transition from 32-bit to 64-bit technology in macOS. iMovie can identify media files that require QuickTime 7 and offers the choice to convert them into a format that is compatible with macOS versions after macOS 10.14. If you decide not to convert the files when initially prompted, iMovie can scan the library at a later time and convert the incompatible files. For a seamless transition, it is important to convert the files before upgrading to the next major version of macOS following macOS 10.14. Once you upgrade, you won't have the option to convert the incompatible media anymore.

Scan the existing library and convert any media that is not compatible

Follow the steps below:

1. To ensure compatibility, open the iMovie app on your Mac and select **File > Check Media for Compatibility**. A window will appear listing any incompatible files found in the library.
2. Click the **Convert button**.

iMovie generates duplicates of the media files in the H.264 format. The original files are relocated to an iMovie Incompatible Media folder, which can be found in the same folder as the library. The original media remains unaltered.

If any missing or incompatible files need additional software

iMovie may detect incompatible files in a library scan. These files cannot be converted due to missing components or the need for additional software. When it comes to that, iMovie conveniently displays a list of the files that are missing or need additional software.

1. Open the iMovie app on your Mac and follow one of these steps:
*   If there are missing incompatible files: Import the clips back into the library.
*   If there are any incompatible files, you may need to install additional software: Ensure that you download and install the necessary software.

CHAPTER FIVE
ADDING AUDIO

Overview

It is nearly impossible to discuss iMovie without talking about how to add audio to your iMovie media. Therefore, in this chapter, you will learn everything that concerns adding audio to iMovie 2024.

Adding audio to iMovie on Mac

Apple is the company that developed the video editing software known as iMovie. Among the capabilities are tools that allow for the modification and optimization of video color settings, the trimming and pivoting of video clips, the smoothing of shaky photos, the addition of video animations, and the modification of their tempo. Additionally, you can modify and improve the audio of a project by removing any background noise and boosting the volume of any quiet sections. iMovie for iOS and macOS allows you to experience your movies in a way that you never have before. It is easy to look through your material and create stunning movies with a quality of 4K. You can also create trailers in the manner of Hollywood. Even better, you may start the editing process on your iPhone or iPad and complete it on your Mac computer. The process of incorporating technology into the film industry has never been simpler, regardless of whether you are using a Mac or an iOS smartphone. To add titles, music, and effects, you need to pick the clips you want to use. Apple's iMovie software even supports 4K video, which enables users to produce films that are of cinematic quality. To put it simply, ladies and gentlemen, that is all there is to it. If you don't have a degree in editing, you can still use iMovie to create videos that appear like they were edited by professionals. A single click allows you to add photographs and videos to projects, you can trim clips with your finger, build immaculate transitions, and fade sounds at a professional level. If you want to add a dramatic touch to your movie, you may choose from thirteen different video filters. You might give the impression that your movie is from the silent period, a classic western, or a comic book that is amusing to read. On your iPhone or iPad, it is simple to apply filters to certain portions of your video or the whole movie, and you can even alter the intensity of the filters. The action movies should be slowed down to make them more intriguing. By speeding up the scenes, you may give viewers the ability to fly through them. As an alternative, you might give your school report the appearance of a broadcast by using methods such as picture-in-picture and split-screen.

Adding Audio to iMovie on an iPhone or iPad: How to Do It?

1. In the project you are working on in iMovie, choose the **ADD MEDIA (+ Symbol) button**.
2. Select **AUDIO** from the menu. Three options will be presented to you at this time. iCloud provides access to songs, soundtracks, and My Music. You are free to choose. To play a

soundtrack, you only need to touch it. If a soundtrack is muted, you should first touch it to download it, and then you should press it again to preview it.

3. Simply click the **Add Audio button** that is located next to the project you want to add a soundtrack to. iMovie will automatically put the music at the beginning of the project and adapt it to meet the length of the project. This will be done throughout the whole project.

Adding sound effects

It is connected to the video clip that is located above it in the timeline when you add a sound effect to the timeline. It is possible to move the sound effects along with the video clip as you move it. However, this is not the same as soundtracks, which are distinct from the video segments that are included in your production. While your project is open, scroll along the timeline until the play head, which is represented by the white vertical line, arrives at the location where you want to add the sound effect.

1. Hit the **Add Media button**, then **Audio**, and finally **Sound Effects** to explore the built-in sound effects.
2. For a sound effect to be heard, touch on it. To include the sound effect, use the Add Audio button that is located next to it.
3. Adjust the volume of the clip. You can adjust the volume of audio clips in your iMovie project to obtain the perfect sound mix or you can adjust the volume of video clips that include sound. Both of these options are available once you have added sound to your project. The volume of an audio or video clip may be altered by selecting it in the timeline, clicking the **Volume button** located at the bottom of the window, and then dragging the slider to increase or decrease the volume depending on your preference. After you have fully decreased the volume of a clip, a Mute sign will appear on the clip in the timeline.

When using iMovie on a Mac, how do you add audio?

You have access to a collection of music and sound clips that are included with iMovie for Mac, which you may utilize in your production. **iMovie contains a variety of audio clips, including ambiances and jingles, in addition to sound effects like rain and footsteps.**

1. While your project is open, go to the top of the browser and pick Audio. After that, select Sound Effects from the sidebar on the left. You may be required to click the button labeled "**Media Browser**" to get access to the Media Browser.
2. You can preview a jingle or sound clip by moving the cursor over it in the list, and then you can play it by clicking the **play button** that is located next to the sound clip. A music or sound clip may also be previewed by choosing it, clicking on the waveform at the top of the media browser, and then hitting the Spacebar. This will allow you to preview the song or sound clip.
3. To generate background music for your film, you can make it by dragging jingles or other audio clips to the music well, which is symbolized by the icon of a musical note on the

timeline. The audio played in the music is not affected in any way by the video clips that are included in the timeline.

4. To include music or sound effects into a video clip, just drag the source file below the video clip until a bar that connects the clips appears. When you move the video clip that is attached, the audio will begin to follow.

How to add audio to iMovie from iTunes

If you want to add tracks such as M4P music and Apple Music from iTunes to iMovie but find that all of the music is protected, all you need is the Sidify Apple Music Converter. Using Sidify Apple songs Converter, you can download songs without experiencing any degradation in quality. Sidify's capacity to remove protection at an incredibly rapid pace – up to twenty times quicker than any other software of its kind – is one of the key benefits that set it apart from other comparable programs. The program has a user interface that is easy to understand. The software is easy to use, even for individuals with little to no prior knowledge. We are going to walk you through the process of adding music from M4P files and Apple Music to an iMovie project so that it may be used as background music.

What you will need is:

- A computer that is either a Mac or a Windows PC that is running either macOS or Windows OS
- The most current version of iTunes.
- There is a Sidify Apple Music Converter accessible for use.
- Play Apple Music using Sidify Apple Music Converter.

Launch the Sidify Apple Music Converter, and then click the plus sign (plus) button. All of the songs that you have downloaded from Apple Music will be shown in the window that allows you to add music, as seen in the image below. Pick the music you want to convert, and then click the OK button.

1. **Choose a file type**

When the user clicks the setting button or the little gear icon located in the top right corner of the Sidify interface, a window that allows them to make adjustments will open. The output formats that you may choose from are MP3, M4A, WAV, FLAC, or AIFF. Additionally, you have the option of selecting a conversion speed of up to 10 times and an output quality of up to 320 kbps. Additionally, the output path can be altered if it is deemed essential to do so.

2. **Start the conversion**

After all of the files have been imported into the queue and all of the configurations have been finished, you should click the Convert button.

3. **Find the music files that have been converted the best for iMovie**

On your Mac computer, you should now click the **Menu button** to identify the converted iTunes Music files in the folder that you have selected. After that, the music may be easily included in an iMovie project in the same way as any other normal audio file would be.

How to add audio from Spotify to iMovie

If you have a Spotify Premium subscription, you can play media offline. It is possible to store songs, playlists, or albums for further listening in the future. It is vital to keep in mind that the Spotify application is the sole means by which users may access music from Spotify, regardless of whether they are connected to the internet or not. To put it another way, you do not have the authorization to import music from Spotify into other software products that are hosted by **third-party developers. Both iMovie and other video editing applications are included in the package.**

1. Soundtracks can be imported into AudFree from Spotify. The AudFree Spotify converter must be compatible with the Music streaming service. Following the execution of the AudFree software from the desktop of your computer, Spotify will instantly begin loading. It is now possible for you to start discovering your favorite songs from Spotify to add to iMovie. The easiest way to import them into AudFree is to either copy and paste them or drag and drop them.

2. iMovie allows you to choose the output format as well as other settings. iMovie is compatible with media formats such as MP3, WAV, M4A, and AIFF. The 'Convert' option can be accessed by going to the top menu and selecting **'Preferences'**. It will then display a window for setup. In the window, you have the option of selecting the output format from among the several audio formats that are supported by iMovie. You also can modify the output settings.

3. Spotify tracks can be transformed so that they can be used in iMovie. It is necessary to click the **'Convert'** button located in the lower-right-hand corner of the main screen to initiate the download. The AudFree application will download music from Spotify to target iMovie files at rates that are up to five times faster than normal. To make the process of converting more reliable, you should deactivate any antivirus or firewall software you may be using.

Adding background music to iMovie on an iMac

The video editing program iMovie is an excellent choice if you are seeking a quick method to include music in your projects. Although it has less functionality than other software, iMovie has a user interface that is straightforward to use, making it an ideal choice for novice professionals. **To add background music to your movie, you will need to follow these instructions if you are working on an iMac:**

1. **Create a new project**

Start by opening your project in iMovie and activating the program. To begin a new iMovie project, first pick **"File"** and then **"Import Media"** from the drop-down menu. You will be able to discover the music that you want to use by using this window that will pop up for browsing. Users can search for certain audio files based on their names, and they may even upload music snippets straight from their iTunes collection.

2. **Integration of the background music**

As soon as you have identified the appropriate track, it is time to include it in your project. When you are adding the music file to your timeline, be sure that it does not overlap any of the video clips that you are working with. When you see a green Add (+) sign, you should no longer hold down the mouse button. This suggests that the music is being inserted as a track that plays in the background of the video. The fact that the track is a background music clip will be indicated by the fact that it will be displayed in green on your timeline. You can easily add background music to particular areas of your movie by dragging the music to the correct beginning point on the timeline. This will allow you to add the music later on. Before releasing the mouse button, it is important to once again search for the green Add (+) sign. Selecting the music clip (the border will become gray) and sliding the slider to either lengthen or reduce the duration of the clip will allow you to make adjustments to the length of the song.

3. **Modify the music in the background**

When using iMovie, you can modify the beginning and ending points of the music that is playing in the background. For example, you could want the music to begin playing in the middle of the song, or you might want to fade it out as the song comes to a close. Click the right mouse button on the music clip, then pick "**Show Clip Trimmer**" and "**Trim to PlayHead**" from the menu that appears. This will provide you the ability to modify the length of time that the background music plays as well as the volume levels during that time. In addition, you can create fade-in and fade-out effects, which provide a smoother transition between the various audio parts.

Record a voiceover in iMovie on Mac

Your narration may be recorded and added to your movie if you so like.

1. Simply move the playhead to the point in the timeline where you want to begin recording, and then click the Record Voiceover button that is located below the viewer in the iMovie application that is installed on your Mac. Below the viewer is where you will find the controls for the voiceover recording.
2. Any one of the following can be done to alter the recording settings:
- **Change the input device:** The input device may be changed by clicking the **Voiceover Options** button ▭▯▭, followed by clicking the **Input Source pop-up menu** and selecting an option from the list of available options.
- **Adjust the input level of the microphone:** Modify the input level of the microphone by clicking the **Voiceover Options button**, and then dragging the loudness slider to the right to raise the loudness of what is being recorded, or to the left to lower it.

By using the audio meter that is located to the left of the red Record button, you can check the levels of the audio. If you want the audio meter to remain green even when your voice is at its loudest, you should adjust the level such that it does not change.
- **Mute sound from other clips while recording**: The Voiceover Options button should be clicked, and the Mute Project option should be selected to muffle the sound of other clips while you are recording.
3. Clicking the **Record button** will begin the recording process.

4. You can stop the recording by clicking the **Record button** once again (or by using the space bar). Above the music that is playing in the background, the audio that was captured is shown as a new clip in the timeline. Additionally, the voiceover clip is tied to the clip that was located below the playhead at the time that the recording was initiated.
5. When you have completed the action, click the **Done button** that is located to the right of the controls for the voiceover recording.

Add audio from a video clip in iMovie on Mac

iMovie will automatically combine audio and video from the same source into a single clip when it is imported. During the process of creating a movie, it is possible to remove the audio from a video clip and then connect it to another clip inside the same movie or to a new movie. In iMovie, the performance of the extracted audio clip is identical to that of any other audio clip. It may be moved, or trimmed, and an audio effect can be applied to it, among other things.

Detach audio from a clip in your movie

1. Select a video clip that has audio in the timeline of the iMovie application that is installed on your Mac.

2. (Alternatively, you can press **Option-Command-B**) Select **Modify > Detach Audio**. Once the audio has been extracted from the video clip, it will be shown as an audio-only clip that is placed below the video clip. This clip will have a green bar. It is now possible to link the audio clip to any other clip in your video, or it may be moved down to the background music well.

Modify the level of the audio in iMovie on a Mac

When you make modifications to the loudness of a clip in iMovie, the audio waveform of the clip will shift into a different shape and color to represent those changes. Make sure that the peak regions of the waveform do not look yellow, which is a sign of distortion, or red, which is a sign of clipping (representing severe distortion). If you see either red or yellow in the waveform of your music, reduce the level until the complete waveform is shown in green. By adjusting the volume of the portion of the waveform that is red or yellow and the remainder of the waveform is green, you can change the color of the waveform.

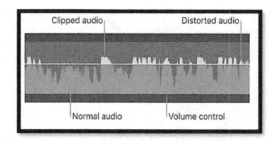

If waveforms are not shown in the timeline, choose the Show Waveforms option by clicking the Settings button located in the upper-right corner of the timeline.

Change the volume in a clip in the timeline

1. Pick an audio clip (or a video clip that includes audio) from the timeline of the iMovie application that you have installed on your Mac.
2. Raise or lower the volume control, which is represented by the horizontal line that runs over the audio waveform. This causes the level to be shown as a % number, and the waveform will change shape to reflect the modifications that you make as you drag.

Change the volume of the part of a clip

One may vary the volume of a specific portion of a clip by selecting a range inside the clip and then adjusting. It is possible to determine the loudness of an audio clip by observing the black horizontal line that runs across the waveform of the audio.

1. While using the iMovie application on your Mac, place the cursor over a clip in the timeline and press and hold the **R key**. When the pointer transforms into the Range Selection pointer ▣, drag over a portion of the clip.
2. Move the volume control, which is represented by the horizontal line in the waveform, up or down within the range that has been set.

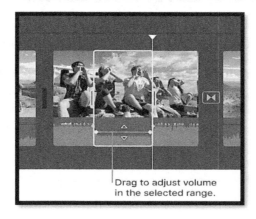

Drag to adjust volume in the selected range.

However, iMovie will automatically add a fade at each boundary of the selection, and the only thing that will be altered is the loudness of the range selection.

Mute the volume

1. Choose one or more audio clips (or video clips that include audio) from the timeline of the iMovie application that is installed on your Mac.
2. To see the volume controls, you must first click the **Volume button**.

3. Select the button labeled "**Mute** ." Click the Mute button once more to unmute the device.

Adjust audio over time with keyframes

Using keyframes, you can lower the level of a portion of a clip and then gradually increase the volume throughout the clip. You can modify the volume at precise places in a clip by adding keyframes, which are markers that you may put at specific positions in the clip. According to the **audio waveform, the relative loudness of the audio clip is represented by the black horizontal line that runs across the waveform.**

1. Using the iMovie application on your Mac, choose a clip from the timeline that includes audio that you wish to modify during the video.
2. Move the cursor to the volume control (the horizontal line) in the waveform area of the clip at the place where you wish to add a keyframe. This will begin the process of adding a keyframe.
3. It is necessary to press and hold the **Option key** when clicking the volume control to add a keyframe.

When you press and hold the **Option key** when the pointer is close to the volume control, the cursor will change to the **Add Keyframe pointer.** It is possible to add as many keyframes to the clip as you like by clicking on them.

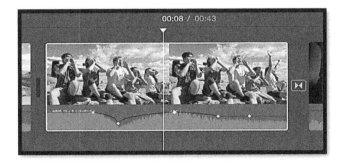

To alter the audio over time, you will need to add at least two keyframes to your clip. This is because any modifications to the volume are performed between two keyframes.

4. Any one of the following should be done after you have added at least two keyframes:
● Use a keyframe to adjust the loudness of the clip by dragging the keyframe in either direction.
● By dragging the volume control between the keyframes in either direction, you may adjust the loudness of the clip that is located between two keyframes.

To remove a keyframe from a clip in the timeline, you must first control-click on the keyframe, and then choose **Delete Keyframe** from the shortcut menu that appears.

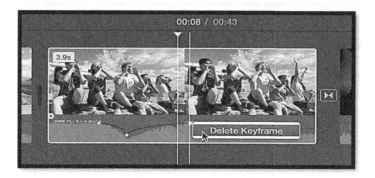

Fade audio in iMovie on Mac

Audio transitions that are often used are called fades. When it comes to audio, fade-ins start with quiet and gradually build to full loudness, whereas fade-outs start at full volume and gradually decline to silence.

1. Place the cursor over the audio part of a clip in the timeline of the iMovie application on your Mac. This will expose the fade handles corresponding to the clip.
2. You can start or stop the fade by dragging a fade handle to the place in the clip where you want it to start or finish.

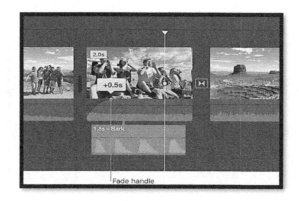

When you drag a fade handle at the beginning of a clip, you produce a fade-in, and when you drag a fade handle after a clip, you make a fade-out.

Correct and enhance audio in iMovie on Mac

iMovie provides you with a variety of options that you may use to improve the audio quality of your video. A clip's quiet audio may have its volume level increased, an equalization setting applied, and background noise reduced. All of these options are available to you.

Automatically enhance audio

1. Choose one or more audio clips (or video clips that include audio) from the timeline of the iMovie application that is installed on your Mac.
2. Simply clicking the **Volume button** will bring up the controls for the volume.

3. Push the button labeled "**Auto**."

When automatic improvements are implemented, the volume of the music in the selection is increased on average, and the Auto button is highlighted to show that the enhancements have been made automatically.

Reduce background noise

In a clip, it is possible to automatically minimize the amount of background noise without lowering the total level of the clip. If you filmed a birthday celebration and an aircraft passed above, for instance, you might lower the volume of the plane to improve the sound quality of your video.

1. Choose one or more audio clips (or video clips that include audio) from the timeline of the iMovie application that is installed on your Mac.
2. By clicking the Noise Reduction and Equalizer button, you will be able to see the controls for noise reduction.

3. The checkbox labeled "**Reduce background noise**" should be selected.

4. You can raise the level of background noise reduction by dragging the slider to the right, or you can take it to the left to lower it. As a percentage of the sound from the original clip, you can alter the amount of background noise reduction. A value of 0% indicates that there is no background noise reduction, while a value of 100% indicates the highest reduction.

5. The footage should be played again to evaluate your change, and then the "**Reduce background noise**" slider should be adjusted to a more precise position.

Apply an equalizer preset

There is a selection of equalizer presets that are included with iMovie, which you can use to improve or correct the audio in your video. As an example, you may choose a preset for the equalization to improve the sound of the vocals, or you can raise the bass or treble in a clip.

1. Choose one or more audio clips (or video clips that include audio) from the timeline of the iMovie application that is installed on your Mac.

2. It is necessary to click the **Noise Reduction** and Equalizer button to see the equalization settings.

3. Choose an equalizer preset by clicking the equalizer pop-up menu with your mouse.

Add audio effects in iMovie on Mac

iMovie comes with a variety of audio effects that may be applied to clips to improve the sound quality of your movies.

Add an audio effect to a clip

1. Choose an audio clip (or a video clip that includes audio) from the browser or timeline of the iMovie application that is installed on your Mac.
2. Clicking the button labeled "**Video and Audio Effects**" will bring up the controls for the effects.

3. You can add an audio effect to the clip by clicking the Audio Effect button and then selecting the effect you want to apply.

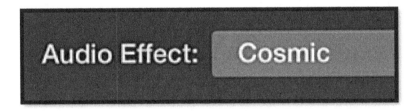

4. To remove an audio effect, you must first choose the clip or range that contains the effect, then click the **Audio Effect button**, and lastly **click All.**

Lower the volume of other clips that play at the same time

Whenever you have a clip playing in the background or other clips with audio playing at the same time as a clip that you want to hear in the forefront, you can automatically reduce the level of the other clips so that they do not compete with the clip that you want to hear. For instance, if you record a portion of the voiceover audio, you can instruct iMovie to reduce the level of the background music and other clips when the voiceover clip is playing.

1. Select a clip in the timeline of the iMovie software on your Mac that has audio that you wish to hear in the foreground after you have made the selection.

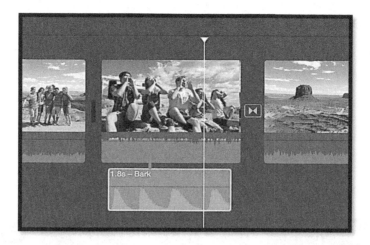

2. Simply clicking the **Volume button** will bring up the controls for the volume.
3. The checkbox labeled "**Lower volume of other clips**" should be selected. Reduced volume is applied to the clips that are not chosen in the playlist.

4. The volume of other clips can be adjusted relative to the loudness of the clip that is currently chosen by dragging the slider.

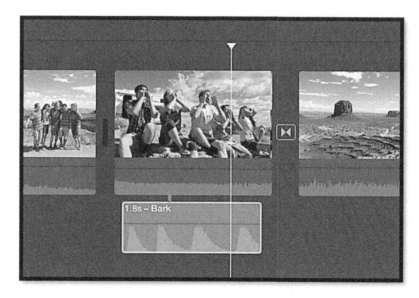

CHAPTER SIX

INCORPORATING TRANSITIONS AND EFFECTS

Overview

Chapter six talks about incorporating transitions and effects into iMovie 2024 including enhancing clips in iMovie, using and applying green screen effects, blurring faces, and even using filters.

Automatically enhance clips in iMovie on Mac

A single click is all that is required to increase the video and audio quality of a clip when you use the **Enhance button** located in the toolbar. When you increase the range of a clip, the modification is applied to the whole clip. This is an important point to keep in mind.

The steps:

1. Choose a clip from the browser or the timeline inside the iMovie application that is installed on your Mac.
2. The Enhance button can be found in the adjustments bar that is located above the viewer. The video and audio in the clip are automatically improved, and some of the other buttons in the adjustments bar, which are often the buttons for color balance and color correction, get highlighted. This indicates that modifications have been performed in the categories that relate to those buttons. If your video clip has audio and may be improved by increasing the volume, the Volume button will also become highlighted by default.

Add video effects in iMovie on Mac

Apple's iMovie software comes with a variety of filters that may be applied to photographs and videos to alter their look. An example of this would be applying a sepia filter to a clip to make it seem as if it was taken from an old film. Additionally, iMovie comes with several preset effect combinations that make it simple to include intricate transitions in your video.

These include:

- **Fade to:** The "**Fade to**" effects are responsible for transforming a clip from its typical look into a black-and-white, sepia, or dreamy appearance.
- **Flash and Freeze Frame**: This effect applies the Ken Burns effect while concurrently including a transition to white and fading in a freeze frame. It also inserts a transition to white.

Add a filter to a clip

1. Choose a clip or range in the browser or the timeline of the iMovie application that is installed on your Mac.
2. The Clip Filter and Audio Effects button should be clicked to see the controls for the effects.

3. Simply choose the filter you want to apply to the clip by clicking the **Clip Filter button,** and then click the filter.

4. Move the slider that is located next to the filter name to the left or right to make adjustments to the filter's strength.

By selecting the clip or range that contains the filter, clicking the **Clip Filter button,** and then clicking **None**, you can remove the filter.

Add a "Fade to" effect

1. Perform one of the following actions inside the iMovie application on your Mac:
- First, choose a clip in the timeline to which you wish to apply the fade effect, and then move the playhead to the point in the timeline where you want the effect to start occurring.

- To apply the fade effect to a specific region in the timeline, you must first choose that range.

If you choose a range, you must leave frames before and after the effect to take into consideration the transitions that are included at the beginning and the conclusion of the effect.

2. To apply an effect, choose **Modify > Fade** and then select an effect from the submenu.

If you pick a whole clip, a fade transition will occur at the location where the playhead is located, and the effect will be applied to the remaining section of the clip. For instance, when you play back a clip that has the Fade to Black and White effect applied, the color fades out at the transition, and the remainder of the clip plays with a black-and-white look. This occurs when you play back the clip. If you have chosen a range, the effect will begin to fade in at the beginning of the range, and it will fade out after the corresponding range.

Add the Flash and Freeze Frame effect

1. Using the iMovie application on your Mac, move the playhead to the point in the timeline of a clip where you want to apply the effect of your choice.
2. Choose the Flash and Freeze Frame option under Modify.

When the clip is played again, it begins to play ahead regularly, and then it fades to white. At that point, the frame that is located at the location of the playhead becomes a freeze frame. Following the application of the Ken Burns effect to the freeze frame, which includes a "**zoom out**," playback resumes as it would usually do when the freeze frame has been completed. After it has been applied, the Ken Burns effect may be altered in some way.

Add transitions in iMovie on Mac

You can create transitions between clips to make the transition from one scene to another more seamless or merge it. A clip can be made to fade in or out, dissolve into another clip, zoom in to another clip, and a variety of additional effects can be applied to it. iMovie allows you to manually create transitions or you may program it to apply transitions automatically according to your preferences.

Add transitions between clips automatically

1. The "**Automatic content**" option can be selected by clicking the Settings button located in the upper-right corner of the timeline inside the iMovie application on your Mac desktop. iMovie will insert conventional cross-dissolve transitions between clips in your video if you have applied a theme to it. Additionally, it may sometimes include transitions that are associated with the theme. There is not a transition put in place for every gap between clips.

In addition, iMovie allows you to put a theme-based opening title over the first clip, as well as an end title over the last clip.

2. After clicking the Theme button, selecting No Theme, clicking Change, and then deselecting the "**Automatic content**" item, you will be able to include just basic transitions that are not themed in your movie.

Note that if you have previously applied a theme to your video and then pick No Theme, all of the components that are associated with the theme will be deleted from the movie.

Add a transition between clips manually

Before you can manually create transitions, you will first need to disable the automated transitions.

1. Begin by opening your video in the timeline of the iMovie software on your Mac, and then pick Transitions from the menu that appears above the browser. To get a sneak peek at a transition, skim it.

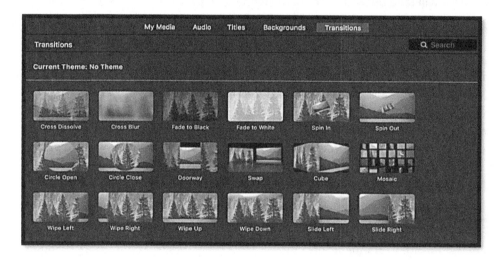

2. **Take one of the following actions:**
- **Add a transition between two clips:** Adding a transition between two clips can be accomplished by dragging a transition between the clips in the timeline's timeline.
- **Add a transition to both ends of a clip**: Adding a transition to both ends of a clip can be accomplished by selecting a clip in the timeline and then double-clicking a transition in the browser toolbar.

In the spaces between the clips, a transition symbol ▶◀ is shown.

Add a cross-dissolve transition between clips

First, you will need to disable automated transitions to create a cross-dissolve transition. This kind of transition is characterized by the first image fading out as the second shot fades in.

1. In the iMovie application on your Mac, locate two clips in the timeline that you wish to join with a cross-dissolve, and then click the edge of either clip. This will achieve the desired connection.

2.   Either hit the Command-T key or choose **Edit > Add Cross Dissolve**.

During the transition between the two clips in the timeline, a cross-dissolve transition is shown. It is important to note that when you choose a clip in the timeline and then click Edit > Add Cross Dissolve, a cross-dissolve technique is applied to both sides of the clip.

Set the default duration of transitions in a movie

iMovie will automatically adjust the duration of all of the transitions in your video to be at the same time. Transitions that are considered standard are one-half of a second long, while transitions that are fashioned after a theme are two seconds long. The theme-styled transitions are only accessible if you have applied a theme to your movie.

1.   Make sure that you choose **iMovie > Settings** from inside the iMovie software on your Mac.
2.   In the Transitions area, double-click the number, and then enter the number of seconds you want to use.

Take note that if the length of your default transition is larger than what is permitted by the media in neighboring clips in your movie, the maximum feasible duration will be utilized instead.

Modify transitions in iMovie on Mac

Change the style of a transition

Before you can manually adjust the style of transitions, you will first need to disable the automated transition process.

1.   Begin by opening your video in the timeline of the iMovie software on your Mac, and then pick Transitions from the menu that appears above the browser. To get a sneak peek at a transition, skim it.

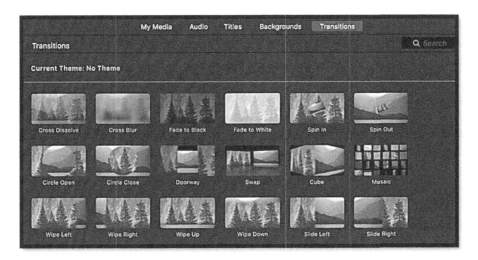

2. Examine the transitions available to locate the new transition that you want to use.

3. Change the transition in the timeline by dragging the new transition to the icon ⏮ that represents the transition you want to replace. The previous transition has been replaced with the new one.

Change the duration of a transition

1. When you are using the iMovie program on your Mac, double-click a transition that is located in the timeline.
2. Double-click the Duration area in the transition controls, and then enter the specific number of seconds you want to use.
3. Select **Apply**.

The length of the transition that you have chosen is modified to match the duration that you have specified. If you provide a number that is longer than what is feasible given the length of the clips that are adjacent to the transition, the duration of the transition will be stretched to the greatest extent possible, and the new duration will be shown in the Duration field. When editing the transition, you can also use the precision editor.

Move a transition

- To add a transition between any two clips in the timeline that do not have a transition, you can use the iMovie software on your Mac to drag a transition between them.

Change all transitions in your movie

Following the application of a transition between clips, you can modify all of the other transitions in your video to be of the same kind and length.

1. You can apply a transition to the rest of the transitions in your movie by double-clicking on it in the timeline of the iMovie program on your Mac. This will include all of the transitions in your movie.
2. Click the **"Apply to all"** button located in the transition controls.

Modify a transition that incorporates several different parts

Certain transitions include components that may be edited by the user. As an example, the transition from Comic Book 3 to Comic Book 4 (which is a component of the Comic Book theme) shows many windows, each of which displays more clips that were utilized in the movie.

1. Choose a transition in the timeline that you wish to alter inside the iMovie application that is installed on your Mac.

Frame markers can appear at different places in the timeline if the transition involves the employment of numerous components. Anchor frames are frames that are used to fill the extra visible clips that are used in the transition. These indicators signify anchor frames.

2. To modify the clips that are used by the transition, you can move the frame markers to other places by dragging them.

The transition uses the clips beginning from the frames that are indicated by the frame markers when it is played back via the player.

How to add effects in iMovie

iMovie is one of the most popular video editing apps for Apple Mac users. It is compatible with both the macOS operating system and the original Mac OS operating system. The addition of iMovie video effects to video clips is one of the most common applications of this program, which was created by Apple and has a history that dates back to 1999. In addition to the ability to change colors, clip video files, rotate them, and stabilize them, iMovie users have access to a wide variety of additional intriguing effects and filters that they may experiment with.

If you want to use video effects with iMovie, you can do it by following the ordered procedures that are listed below:

1. At the outset, you will be required to download iMovie, after which you will proceed to install and open the application. After the software has been opened, you will need to choose File and then Import to begin the process of importing the video file or files that you want to have access to. When using iMovie, users can import a wide variety of video formats, including MPEG, DV, and HDV.

2. When you have finished importing your movies, go to the Project Library selection and click on a clip that you want to apply iMovie effects to. It will look like a Gear symbol is there, and you may use it to click on the Clip Adjustments option. After that, a window labeled "**Inspector**" will emerge, and it will include the text "**Video Effect: None.**"

3. To access the collection of free iMovie effects and iMovie filter options, you can access the library by clicking on the Video Effect icon. It is possible to learn more about the various effects by hovering your mouse over them. Once you have done so, you can click on a video effect in iMovie that you would want to employ to include it in your content.

4. In iMovie, after you have finished applying your new effect, you will return to the main dashboard area, and you will be able to preview the effect in the window that is located in the upper right corner of the screen. Following that, you have the option of downloading more iMovie filters to your movie, if you so wish, or you can just save and export your file if you are satisfied with the outcome.

iMovie Effects

Within iMovie, users have access to a wide variety of effects, some of which include the following:

- **Color adjustments**: iMovie users can modify or improve the colors of each clip that they use.
- **Crop**: You can trim your clips to modify their size and get rid of distracting aspects.
- **Rotate**: There are also a variety of angles at which clips may be turned.
- **Stabilize**: Shaky Videos can be stabilized to provide a watching experience that is more clear and uncluttered.
- **Transitions**: Your transition from one clip to another in iMovie is made possible by a wide variety of transitions, such as the iMovie fade-in or fade-out transitions.
- **Speed**: It is also possible to alter the pace of clips to produce a slow-motion or fast-motion effect.
- **Filters**: The look of the video graphics may be altered with the use of a wide variety of filters, such as a black and white or vintage filter.
- **Green screen**: Users can modify the backdrop of their files and remove a topic from their files by using the green screen effect.
- **Split screen:** As an additional option, files may be presented in split-screen mode.

- **Picture-in-picture**: Through the use of this effect, it is possible to show two photographs at the same time.
- **Audio**: There are a variety of audio effects that may be used to improve the sound quality or to create additional audio tracks.

Frequently Asked Questions in adding Effects

Does iMovie support the addition of animations?

While using iMovie, it is possible to include animations in the video files you have created. To begin, you will need to click on the "**Create a New Movie**" button and then import the video files that you want to work with. Immediately after that, you will also be required to import the animated graphic that you want to work with. Once you have arrived at that point, all that is required of you is to drag and drop the video file into the working area, and then put the animation effects on top of it.

Does iMovie have any effects that you can use?

You are going to need to locate the Effects option to make the most of the effects that are available in iMovie. This button is located in the main menu area, just below the video clips that you have uploaded. When you click on this option, a new menu will emerge with all of your clips. You can then click on the clip that you want to add effects to, and the effects menu will appear. From there, you will be able to apply effects such as fade-in, page curl, and other similar effects.

In iMovie, is it possible to add sound effects?

Users of iMovie can include musical backdrops and audio effects in their video files. You have the option of importing audio from other libraries on your device, or you may pick from the software's collection of sound files that are included in the package. You have the option of adding background music or effects, and they will play in combination with the audio that is already included in your files.

In iMovie, how can I adjust the effects that run on videos?

In this regard, it is dependent on the kind of video effect that you are dealing with. There are certain effects that you won't be able to change since iMovie does not let users personalize all of the numerous effects using the program. When applying these effects, however, some ones, such as the Green Screen effect, may be modified according to the requirements via the menus that are supplied.

How to Use iMovie Green Screen

By shooting the movie with a backdrop of blue or green hue, you will have the ability to swap the background with other sceneries that are intriguing and compelling. On the other hand, if you do not include the green screen backdrop in the process of generating the film, the quality of the video may suffer when the background is edited. If you film a movie with a single-colored backdrop (often green or blue), the green screen effect in iMovie gives you the ability to make that color translucent. If you so like, you are free to substitute the backdrop with any other video clip, graphic, or still picture of your own. You can easily superimpose anything into any shot by using the green screen effect that is available in iMovie. You can go to any location you like or to play a role in the films that you enjoy the most. How can I use iMovie to create a green screen? To apply the green screen effect in iMovie, you will now need to follow the instructions. While you are in the process of making a film with a green screen, one of the most notable possibilities that you may consider is the green screen that is available in iMovie.

How do you do an iMovie Green Screen?

Having a conversation about the qualifications of the iMovie is essential before looking at the green screen in iMovie. Almost every parameter may be edited with great effect with this superb video editing tool, which gives you the ability to customize the film remarkably. Even though iMovie does not provide the most intuitive and user-friendly interfaces, it is possible to acquire previous knowledge of this program in a short amount of time. It not only allows you to edit the different components of the film, but it also gives you the luxury of using the green screen feature that is available in iMovie. Using this method, you may give the impression that you are producing the movie in iMovie using a green screen, which will make the film more relevant and magnificent.

Learning how to use the green screen in iMovie is broken down into a series of steps that are shown below.

1. To begin, you will need to open iMovie and then choose the **File icon** from the menu. Following the selection of the File option, you will be required to press the **Import button** to upload the green screen and background movie. Before you submit a movie to iMovie, you need to make sure that it is compatible with the program. If this does not occur, you will be unable to edit the films in iMovie. The **"Event Browser"** also allow you to drag your movie to the Project Library at any time.

In this stage, you will have the opportunity to include the background clip into your timeline. Additionally, you can edit, crop, and alter the background video or picture to meet your specific needs. After clicking the green screen button, the next step is to move the video that is being shown on the green screen to the timeline.

2. When you are editing two different bits of film, you will need to make sure that they are of the same length. After you have visited the timeline, you should tap on the green screen film; a yellow box will indicate that it is there. The Green/Blue Screen option can be selected by navigating to your preview window, tapping the "**Video Overlay Settings**" option, and then selecting the choice. Since this is the case, you will be able to see the true magic. By using the Cleanup and Softness tools, you are also able to personalize the approach to improve the final product.

As soon as you have completed all of these procedures, you will be able to apply the green screen in iMovie using an incredible method.

Create a green-screen effect in iMovie on Mac

The subject of the video can be **"cut out"** and superimposed over another video clip after it has been recorded in front of a green or blue background. An effect like this is referred to as a green-screen or blue-screen effect. As an example, you might videotape a buddy dancing in front of a green or blue background, and then overlay that video over a clip displaying a starry sky. This would give the impression that your friend is dancing in the sky. Additionally, you have the option of dragging the green-screen or blue-screen clip over a backdrop clip that is either solid-colored or animated. It is recommended that you film your video in front of a blue backdrop if the subject of your movie is green or if you are wearing green clothing. It is also recommended that you film your video in front of a green backdrop if the topic of your video is wearing blue or if the subject is wearing blue. When the green-screen or blue-screen clip is played, the audio from the original clip and the audio from the clip that was played concurrently are played. You can lower the level of either clip to make the sound from the other clip more noticeable.

Create an effect using a green screen or a blue screen

1. When you are using the iMovie application on your Mac, choose a clip or range in the timeline that you filmed against a green or blue background, and then drag it over a clip that is already present in your project. You should let go of the mouse button when you see the **green Add symbol** on the screen.

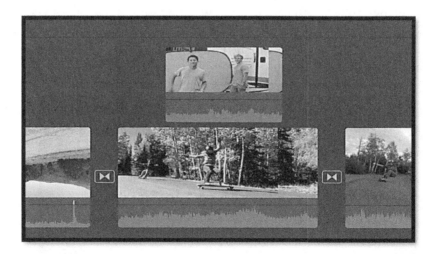

2. The Video Overlay Settings button should be clicked if the video overlay controls are not shown.

3. Select **Green/Blue Screen** from the pop-up option that appears on the left side of the screen.

The clip that was filmed against the green or blue background gets the green or blue removed from it in the viewer, and the clip that is below it shows through the sections that were green or blue, therefore generating a composite picture. When you choose **Green/Blue Screen** from the pop-up menu, the color that is removed by iMovie is determined by the color that is most prominent in the frame at the point where the playhead is located. There is a possibility that you will need to relocate the playhead and reapply the effect if the frame that is located below the playhead does not accurately reflect the remainder of the clip. Simply dragging the green-screen or blue-screen clip to a new location inside the clip or to a separate clip will allow you to relocate one of these clips. It is also possible to drag the ends to extend or shorten it.

4. Simply click the **Apply button** located under the Green/Blue Screen controls to put the changes into effect.

Modify a green-screen or blue-screen effect

The steps:

1. When using the iMovie application on your Mac, choose a clip in the timeline that has either a green screen or a blue screen.
2. The Video Overlay Settings button should be clicked if the Green/Blue Screen controls are not shown.

3. **Carry out any of the following:**
- **Adjust the softness of the edges of the superimposed clip**: By dragging the Softness slider, you can adjust the degree of softness that the borders of the overlay clip feature.

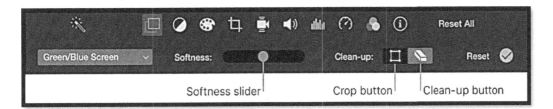

- **Isolate areas of the green-screen or blue-screen clip**: The subject in the foreground clip can be isolated by clicking the **Crop button** and then dragging the edges of the frame. This will allow you to isolate certain portions of the green-screen or blue-screen clip of your choice.
- **Clean up areas of the green-screen or blue-screen clip**: To clean up areas of the green-screen or blue-screen footage, you must first click the **Clean-up button** and then drag over any stray bits of the green-screen or blue-screen clip that should not be shown.

When you drag, iMovie uses the new selection to decide what should be cleaned up. This happens every time you drag. Before you click the **Clean-up button**, you should make sure that the Softness setting is selected. The backdrop clean-up option will be reset and will need to be reselected if you make any adjustments to the Softness setting after you have used the Clean-up button.

4. Click the **Apply button** located under the Green/Blue Screen controls to put the modification into effect.

Create a split-screen effect in iMovie on Mac

With the use of a split-screen effect, it is possible to include a clip into another clip to have both clips play simultaneously. Additionally, you have the option of selecting whether the attached clip glides into the frame or if it presents itself in the left, right, top, or bottom of the frame. The length of a slide-in transition may be customized if you want to include one.

Create a split-screen clip

1. Using the iMovie program on your Mac, choose a clip or range that you wish to display at the same time as another clip, and then drag it over a clip in the timeline. This will allow you to show the clips simultaneously. You should let go of the mouse button when you see the green Add symbol on the screen.

2. If the controls for the video overlay are not shown, click the button labeled "**Video Overlay Settings**."

3. The next step is to choose **Split Screen** from the pop-up menu that appears on the left. The split-screen controls mode is shown above the viewer, and copies of both videos that have been cropped are displayed inside itself.

Drag the split-screen clip in the timeline so that it links to a new location in the clip below, or drag it to a different clip, to vary the moment at which the split-screen effect emerges. It is also possible to drag the ends to extend or shorten it.

4. To put the change into effect, choose the split-screen controls and then click the **Apply button**.

Adjust a split-screen clip

1. First of all, choose a clip that is split-screen in the timeline of the iMovie application that is installed on your Mac.
2. Click the button labeled "**Video Overlay Settings**" if the split-screen controls are not automatically shown.
3. **Choose one of the below options:**
- The position of the attached clip in the frame may be adjusted as follows: Once the pop-up menu for Position appears, choose an option from the list.
- Add a transition that slides in, and determine how long it will last: Slide the slider to the right.

If you set the transition length to 0, there will be no transition that takes place.

4. To put the modifications into effect, choose the split-screen controls and then click the Apply button.

How to blur faces

Most of the time, a large number of individuals are susceptible to identity theft. Additionally, there are instances in which exposing the faces of rape victims might reveal their genuine identity to the public, which is something that should be kept hidden. There are a variety of technologies that may blur faces and conceal the identity of a person when films are shown on television. These tools are often used frequently. This blurring capability is especially helpful for concealing sensitive information, such as the number plates of automobiles, financial information, and other similar items that should not be released to the general public. Although blurring faces in iMovie is a challenging process, we will make an effort to explain it in the following part. You are going to need to make advantage of the picture-in-picture functionality to blur the face.

Proceed with the actions that are listed below:

1. Launching the iMovie app is the first step, which can be accomplished by clicking **iMovie > Preferences**. When you have finished doing this, choose the general setting, turn on the Show Advanced Tools option, and then shut the iMovie interface.

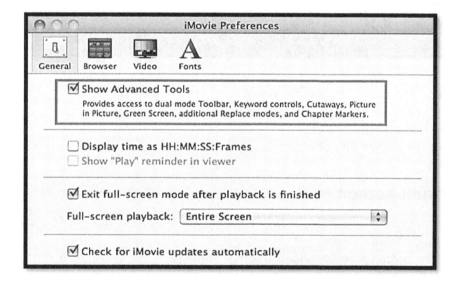

2. The selection of the video clip that will be shown on the license plate is the first step in the second stage. Following that, the video clip will be shown to the viewer of iMovie.
3. Using the Shift key + Command + 4, take a snapshot of the face. After you have finished with it, you should let go of the mouse button. When the screenshot has been taken and stored on your desktop, you will hear a shutter sound. This will prove that the screenshot has been successfully recorded.

4. At this point, you need to open it in any image editor, such as Photoshop or Gaussian, which might cause your picture to become blurry. You can make whatever modification to it that you like. Save your picture to the desktop when you have finished making changes to it.

5. Move it over the clip you have in iMovie, and then pick Picture in Picture from the option that displays. After you have finished this process, the picture that has been blurred will be shown as a still in the viewer as well as in the project pane of iMovie.

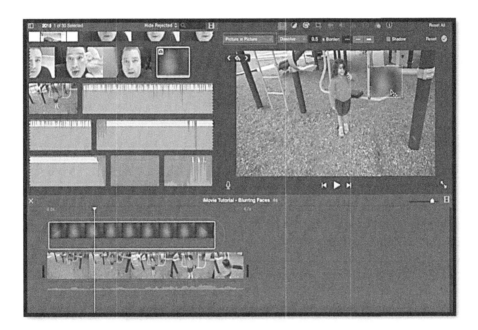

6. Now, modify the length of the clip so that it will cover the license plate for the whole of the clip's duration.

7. The last step involves scaling the picture and positioning it accordingly in the spot that you have chosen.

FAQs Regarding the Blurring of Faces in iMovie

They include the following:

In iMovie, is it possible to blur faces?

This is a very sophisticated procedure, but yes, you can do it. To add the blur effect to the still frame that you saved from iMovie, you will need to have access to picture editing tools such as Adobe Photoshop. Following that, you will be able to conceal a face in your video by using the Picture in Picture tool.

In iMovie, how do I blur out numerous faces at the same time?

There is no difference in the method that is used to blur one or more faces in iMovie. It might be beneficial if you exported still frames that include the faces that you want to blur out, then used a picture editing program to apply the blur effect over those faces, then finally used the Picture in Picture tool in iMovie to blur out the faces in your film. The only drawback is that you will have to go through this procedure for every single shot in case you wish to blur out many faces.

What are the steps to blurring faces in iMovie on an iPad?

The procedures that you need to do to blur a face in iMovie are the same whether you are using a Mac, an iPhone, or an iPad. This means that you will need to generate a still frame, apply the blur effect to it in a picture editing program, and then utilize the Picture in Picture function of iMovie to cover a face.

How to add filters in iMovie

During the process of video editing, you can apply a variety of effects to your film by using iMovie Filters. Many different types of iMovie filters are available for use to modify the coloration of the video clips and add unique effects to them. You may not even notice the iMovie filters, however when compared to the other important tools that are available in iMovie.

1. **First of all, import videos to iMovie**

Initiate iMovie, open the project you are working on, or begin a new project. To import video clips, click on the **File menu** and then select the **Import option**.

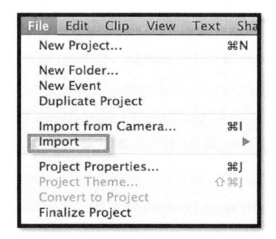

It is important to note that iMovie is compatible with the following video formats: DV, DV Widescreen, HDV 1080i (25 and 30 frames per second), HDV 720p (25 and 30 frames per second), MPEG 4 Simple Profile, and iSight. Several camcorder models are not supported by the software. Before you import movies into iMovie, check to see whether the films you want to import are compatible with iMovie. need this not be the case, you need to purchase a Mac video converter to convert films and DVDs to iMovie.

2. **Add Video Effects to iMovie**

When you choose a video clip from the Project Library, you will notice that a "**Gear**" appears on the screen. Select the "**Clip Adjustments**" option. Following that, an "**Inspector**" icon will appear on the screen for you to see. "**None**" is shown in this window for the Video Effect property. The Video Effect button in iMovie is where you should click to add a video effect. After clicking this button, you will be presented with a selection of video effects from which you may choose one. You can preview each effect by moving your cursor over it. Locate the specific one that you think is appealing, and then click on it to add it to your clip.

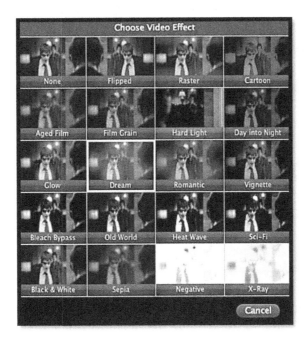

3. **Preview the Result**

You will be able to preview your movies in the viewing window after you have selected the video effect. This will allow you to see the effect in its entirety. You can change the video effect in any way you see fit if you are not content with it. After ensuring that everything is in order, you can proceed to complete it by pressing the "**Done**" button.

Create a cutaway effect in iMovie on Mac

You can choose to put a cutaway clip on top of another clip to demonstrate two distinct points of view about the same incident. As an example, you can show someone preparing to join a surprise party, and then cut away to a shot of the others waiting inside the celebration. It is important to note that the time of your movie will not be altered in any way when you add a cutaway clip since it will cover an equal percentage of the video clip that you added it to.

Add a cutaway clip

- Create a cutaway clip by selecting a clip or range that you wish to cut away to in the iMovie software on your Mac, and then dragging it over a clip in the timeline. This will create a cutaway clip.

While you are dragging the clip, the cursor will change to the green **Add icon (+),** and a line will emerge linking the clip that you are dragging to the clip that is located in the timeline.

Let go of the mouse button after the clip has been positioned exactly where you want it to be. Drag the cutaway clip to a new location inside the clip or to a separate clip to relocate it after it has been removed. It is also possible to drag the ends to extend or shorten it. You can also create a cutaway by dragging a clip that is already in the timeline over another clip that is in the timeline.

Adjust the fades in a cutaway clip

Customize the length of time that a cutaway clip dissolves in and out, as well as set it to dissolve in and out.

1. Within the iMovie application on your Mac, choose a cutaway clip from the timeline that you want to modify or modify differently.
2. If the controls for the video overlay are not shown, click the button labeled "**Video Overlay Settings.**"

3. **Choose one of the below options:**
- **Use the cutaway settings to choose the length of the fade**: Move the slider labeled "Fade."
- **Set the fade duration in the timeline**: You can adjust the duration of the fade by dragging one of the fade handles located at the top of the cutaway clip toward the center of the clip. If you want to shorten the fade, you can drag it toward the edge of the clip.

4. To put the modification into effect, choose the cutaway controls and then click the **Apply button**.

CHAPTER SEVEN
ADDING PHOTOS AND GRAPHICS

Overview

Chapter seven brings us to learning how to add photos and graphics to iMovie 2024. Here, you will see how to create a photomontage, the various supported image formats, and others.

How to create a photomontage

No matter the occasion - be it a family reunion, rehearsal dinner, or business event - a photomontage is a fantastic addition that will surely entertain and inform. The Mac's iMovie software seamlessly integrates with the Photos application, allowing you to create a photomontage that exudes professionalism and fills you with pride. The Photos application comes pre-installed on all Macs, while iMovie is available at no cost for Mac users. If iMovie is not already installed on your computer, you can easily download it from the Mac App Store for free.

Transform Your Photos into Digital Format

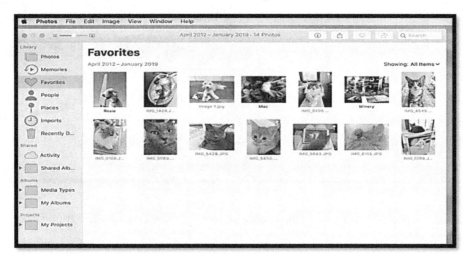

Before starting the process of creating a photomontage, it is essential to have digital copies of all the pictures you intend to use on your Mac. If the images are sourced from a digital camera or if you have already scanned and saved them in Photos, then you are good to go. If you're working with standard photo prints, you can easily digitize them at home using a scanner. If you lack a scanner or have a large number of pictures, a nearby photography store can assist you in digitizing them. For a more efficient montage-making process, consolidate all the chosen photos into a single album in the Photos app and give it a memorable name, like the iMovie album.

Alternatively, you can effortlessly browse through Photos and choose the ones you wish to use at random.

Launch iMovie

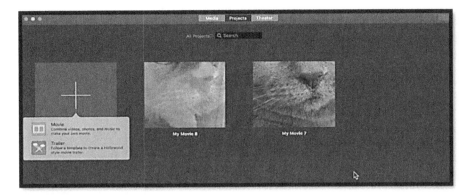

To start, open iMovie and choose **New Movie** from the **File menu** located at the top of the screen. Alternatively, you can use the keyboard shortcut **Command + n**. Open the iMovie screen and navigate to the Projects tab. Look for the Create New icon, which is marked with a large plus sign. Select a movie from the pop-up window.

Open the Photos App

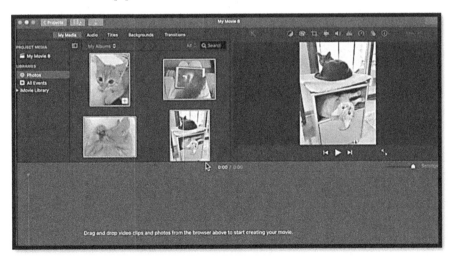

To access your photos in iMovie, go to the project screen and click on the **My Media tab**. Then, navigate to the Libraries section on the left side of the main work area and select Photos. You can open the Photos library previews in iMovie and easily select the pictures you want to include in the montage. You can choose them from a saved iMovie album or browse through your Photo albums and select individual images.

Arrange the Photos in the Timeline

Select each image by clicking on it. Then drag the selected photos to the timeline located at the bottom of the screen. Drag and drop each photo to rearrange their order as you please.

Choose Ken Burns

Use the Ken Burns effect to incorporate dynamic movement into the images. To activate the Ken Burns controls, simply select the first photo and click on the crop icon located above the preview screen at the top of the iMovie window. Click on the image in the preview window and position the Start box and the End box in two different positions on the photo. Complete this process for every photo and then select the play control beneath the preview window to observe the impact. It may require some experimentation, but you can fine-tune each image until you are satisfied with the desired outcome. To preview your photo montage effects, simply move the playhead to just before the first photo on the timeline and click the play control below the preview window.

Include a Transition

There are various effects that you can use for your photomontage. Transitions effects help create a seamless flow between photos. The selection of transitions in iMovie is quite extensive, but the Cross Dissolve is a subtle option that seamlessly blends still images together without drawing too much focus. To apply a cross-dissolve effect, first, select all the images on the timeline. Then, navigate to the menu bar and click on **Edit**. From the options that appear, choose **Add Cross Dissolve**. To see how it looks, simply click the play button located below the preview screen. You have the option to adjust the cross-dissolve time by clicking on the icon that appears between each image and inputting your desired number of seconds.

Add a Title

To access a variety of title styles, go to the Titles tab at the top of the screen and choose **Content Library > Titles**. This will open up previews for you to explore. Once you've discovered a title style that appeals to you, simply position the playhead in the desired spot on the timeline. Typically, this is at the beginning of the video where you want the title to make its appearance. Click on your preferred title style and enter the title in the preview window, replacing the placeholder text. A title screen has been included in the timeline.

Fade to Black

To access the Transitions menu, navigate to **Window > Content Library > Transitions** or simply click on the **Transitions tab**. The addition of a Fade Out, found within the Transitions, provides a graceful conclusion to the video. After the pictures are done, you'll be left with a black screen instead of a frozen final frame of video. Place this effect at the end of the montage, following the same steps used for the title and picture dissolves. Locate the playhead and select Fade to Black from the transitions options.

Remember to include the audio

Once you have perfected your photos and effects to your satisfaction, take a moment to enhance your photomontage with some background music. To choose a tune, simply navigate to the **Audio tab** and select an option from the menu that appears. Simply click and drag the song to the timeline below the photos. To ensure a seamless transition, simply scroll to the end of the music track, click on it, and drag it back to a point beyond the last photo.

Final Steps

Now is the perfect moment to put your photomontage to the test. Position the playhead right before the initial photo on the timeline. Ensure that all the picture effects, transitions, and titles are visually appealing by clicking the play control under the preview window and watching the photomontage from beginning to end. If there's anything you'd like to modify, now is the perfect opportunity. As you work on your project, iMovie automatically saves it for you. When you're ready to share your photomontage, simply click on File > Share and choose from a variety of options such as Email, iTunes, YouTube, and more. Navigate to the Projects tab located at the top of the iMovie screen. Enter a title in the designated field that appears, which will take you back to the main iMovie screen.

Supported image formats

Which file formats are compatible with iMovie?

The issue of media format compatibility remains a global challenge that has yet to be resolved. Thankfully, the situation has improved compared to previous decades. The MP4 format with h264 video and ACC audio is currently the most widely supported file format. There should be no issue importing your videos into iMovie for editing if they are saved in these formats. Nevertheless, the real world is always complex. There are numerous video formats available worldwide. The format of video files can vary depending on how they were obtained. Take a look at the list below, which showcases the different formats offered by Apple. iMovie for Mac from Catalina supports a variety of video formats, container formats, audio formats, and image formats. It's worth noting that older versions of iMovie may have varying supported formats. It is important to test the video import functionality in iMovie to ensure a successful import.

Video formats	Container formats	Audio formats	Still-image formats
• Apple Animation Codec	• 3GP	• AAC	• BMP
• Apple Intermediate Codec	• AVI	• AIFF	• GIF
• Apple ProRes	• M4V	• BWF	• HEIF
• AVCHD	• MOV (QuickTime)	• CAF	• JPEG
• DV	• MP4	• MP3	• PNG
• H.264		• MP4	• PSD
• HDV		• RF64	• RAW
• HEVC		• WAV	• TGA
• iFrame			• TIFF
• Motion JPEG (OpenDML)			
• MPEG-4 SP			
• Photo JPEG			
• XAVC-S			

To convert an incompatible file, simply open it with QuickTime Player (version 10.0 and later) and save a copy with a different name. Unfortunately, this method is not compatible with macOS Catalina or later. In addition, Compressor offers the ability to convert files into various formats including H.264, HEVC, or Apple ProRes. The table above clearly shows the supported formats in different versions of iMovie. H.264 and HEVC maintain video quality while minimizing file size. The video quality of ProRes is exceptional and it offers superior performance when editing in iMovie. However, it is worth noting that the file size of ProRes is significantly larger compared to H.264 and HEVC files. If you're looking to convert iMovie-incompatible media files, another option is Movavi Video Converter, which is compatible with both Mac and Windows operating systems.

Video Formats Supported by iMovie for Importing

iMovie is an excellent video editing application created by Apple, specifically for those who are new to video editing. Unfortunately, there are several reasons, such as copyright restrictions, that prevent certain videos from being imported into iMovie. It is important to be aware of the supported formats for importing in iMovie, as well as the incompatible formats that are commonly encountered.

Supported Formats for iMovie

The available video codecs include Apple Animation Codec, Apple Intermediate Codec (AIC), Apple ProRes, AVCHD (including AVCCAM, AVCHD Lite, and NXCAM), DV (including DVCAM, DVCPRO, and DVCPRO50), H.264, HDV, H265/HEVC, iFrame, Motion JPEG (OpenDML only), MPEG-4 SP, and XAVC-S.

- Supported container formats include MOV (QuickTime), MP4, 3GP, and AVI (as long as they contain supported codecs). M4V is also supported.
- The available audio codecs include AAC, AIFF, BWF, CAF, MP3, MP4, RF64, and WAV.
- The supported still image formats include BMP, GIF, HEIF, JPEG, PNG, PSD, RAW, TGA, and TIFF.

Incompatible Formats in iMovie

- **WMV**: Windows Media Video, a video format developed by Microsoft.
- **AVI**: Introduced by Microsoft, AVI stands for Audio Video Interleaved.
- **FLV**: Developed by Adobe, the widely utilized Adobe Flash Player.
- **MKV**: This is a description of Matroska Video, a container format that is open-source and can be used on different platforms.
- **VOB**: Video OBject, commonly abbreviated as VOB, is a term often associated with DVDs.
- **WebM**: A file container format introduced by Google, which is similar to the MKV format.

Be aware that this is not an exhaustive list. It contains commonly used formats in everyday situations. If you want to import media files into iMovie that are not supported by the software, you will need a reliable video converter designed for Mac. With just 3 simple steps, you can easily make your media files fully compatible with iMovie. All you need to do is import your files, select an output format, and start the video conversion process right away.

Video Formats Supported by iMovie for Exporting

The amount of custom space provided by iMovie for sharing your movies is insufficient. It can vary depending on your specific requirements. For instance, iMovie does not support exporting WMV files, making it difficult to share them with friends who use Windows. Take a look at the table below for an introduction to iMovie export formats.

Export Formats for iMovie

- **QuickTime File**: Export your iMovie project to a QuickTime file, which can include both video and audio or just audio. The choice between MOV or MP4 will depend on the selected Quality option. By selecting Low, Medium, or High, the exported file will be saved in MP4 format. The exported file will be in MOV format if you choose Best (ProRes). If necessary, you can consider converting it to other formats such as AVI. Keep in mind that iMovie seamlessly supports 4K video.
- **Online**: Upload your videos directly to YouTube, Facebook, and Vimeo with ease.

- **iTunes**: Add your iMovie video to the Movies section of your iTunes library. It is compatible with Apple TV, iPad, iPhone, or iPod touch for convenient viewing.
- **Email**: Send your movie or trailer via email using Mail, the macOS email application.
- **Image**: Export a JPEG file from a frame of video in your movie.
- **Theater**: iMovie 10 or later no longer supports sharing to iMovie Theater. The Photos APP is highly recommended for watching and managing your movies.

Common Questions about iMovie Formats

What are the most suitable formats for iMovie video editing?

Apple recommends using Apple Intermediate Codec and Apple ProRes for video editing with iMovie, Final Cut Express, and Final Cut Pro up to version 5. ProRes has become a common choice after the release of Final Cut Pro 6. Apple Intermediate Codec is a highly efficient format for iMovie, as it requires less processing power to work with. AIC serves as an intermediary format within an HDV and AVCHD workflow. Although it is possible to import a video to iMovie, it is not advisable to convert it to Apple Intermediate Codec. This is because each conversion will inevitably impact the original quality of your video. For instance, iMovie is capable of editing H264 videos in MP4 format. No need to convert it to AIC. However, if you're working with a video that is not compatible with iMovie, it is advisable to use the AIC format instead of H264. This is because H264 is primarily designed for playback purposes rather than editing.

Is there a way to determine if a format is compatible with iMovie?

The QuickTime Player can be used to easily determine if a video is compatible with iMovie. If the video plays smoothly, it is possible to edit it using iMovie. To use it in iMovie, you will need to convert the video to a compatible format such as Apple Intermediate Codec in MOV or MP4 file container. We highly recommend using Movavi Video Converter for Mac. The software is capable of converting videos to a format that is compatible with iMovie while maintaining the original quality. For a seamless video editing experience on Mac, consider using Movavi Video Editor. It eliminates any compatibility issues and allows you to edit videos effortlessly.

Avoid using these formats on your Mac anymore - here are some tips on iMovie formats

Apple is currently focused on transitioning from 32-bit to 64-bit technology. This transition will also have an impact on media formats. Below are the formats that iMovie 10, iMovie '11, or other versions of iMovie may support. Although it may not be compatible with future versions of iMovie. It is advisable to steer clear of using these formats in iMovie to prevent potential issues with compatibility down the line. The following codecs are supported: 3ivx MPEG-4, AV1 / VP9, BitJazz SheerVideo, CineForm, Cinepak, Flash Video, FlashPix, FLC, H.261, Implode, Indeo video 5.1, Intel Video 4:3, JPEG 2000, Microsoft Video 1, Motion JPEG A, Motion JPEG B, On2 VP3, VP5, VP6, VP6-

E, VP6-S, VP7, VP8, VP9, Perian collection of codecs (Microsoft MPEG-4, DivX, 3ivx, VP6, VP3, and others), Pixlet, Planar RGB, RealVideo, Sorenson 3, Sorenson Sparc, Sorenson Video / Video 3 / YUV9, Streambox ACT-L2, Windows Media Video 7, 8, 9, Xiph.org's Theora Video, ZyGoVideo.

Creating stop motion and time-lapse videos in iMovie

Stop motion is a highly enjoyable effect that you may come across in the work of other individuals from time to time. Stop motion, also known as Stop Frame Animation, is a captivating technique used in both 2D and 3D animation. It creates the mesmerizing illusion of objects coming to life and moving on their own. Stop motion can be seen as both captivating and intricate. Although slow motion requires more effort compared to other techniques like time-lapse, iMovie's stop motion feature can make the process easier. Let's use the latest version of iMovie, iMovie 10, as an example to demonstrate how to create a stop-motion video. Before creating a slow-motion video, it is crucial to thoroughly plan the storyline and capture all the necessary images for your video.

1. First, open iMovie and import all the media files you plan to use for your stop-motion video. Make sure to arrange them in the correct sequential order.

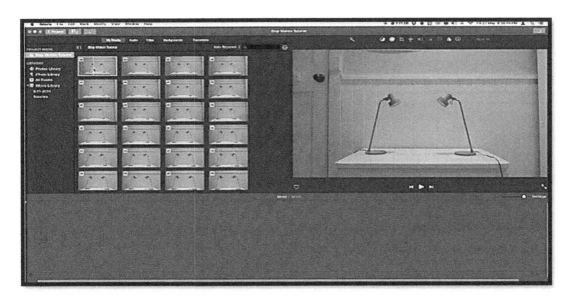

2. Proceed to iMovie and choose "**Preferences**". Modify the "**Photo Placement**" setting to "**Fit in Frame**" to maintain the desired stop motion effect while zooming in and out on your images.

3. Arrange all the photos in a neat order and drag them to the timeline. Please adjust the duration of each photo. The suggested duration is 0.1 seconds, resulting in a smooth stop-motion sequence at a rate of 10fps. Ensure that this is applied to all photos. It is possible to extend the duration of a specific photo to your desired length.

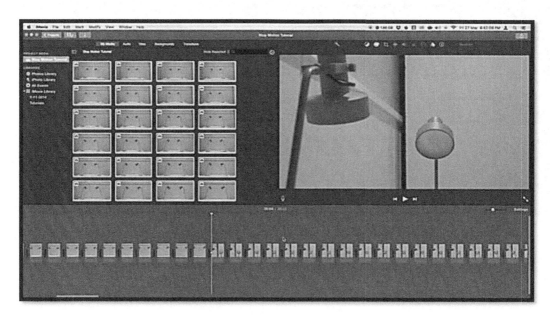

4. After completing Step 3, you can export the stop motion video and easily incorporate it into your project for future use.

Here's an alternative approach:

Stop motion and time-lapse can add a playful touch to your video editing projects. Some people may believe that they require sophisticated software or expensive video editing programs to complete the task. With some know-how, even iMovie can be used to create slow-motion and time-lapse videos.

Step-by-step instructions for creating a stop motion or time-lapse sequence in iMovie are provided below:

1. Launch iMovie. Navigate to Properties and then select Timing. Modify the preferences to switch from "**Ken Burns**" to "**Fit in Frame**". Your photos will remain steady and consistent throughout the stop-motion effect.
2. If all of your photos are already in sequential order, simply click and drag them into iMovie.
3. Modify the length of each clip. To accomplish this, simply double-click on one of the images. Here's how you can bring up the inspector window. Reduce the duration to 0.1 seconds instead of 4 seconds. Make sure to apply this to all the stills. This will enable your stop-motion sequence to move at a rate of 10 frames per second, which is the maximum speed allowed by iMovie.
4. Export the video. You can easily connect multiple stop clips to create different scenes.
5. Include your stop motion clip in your project and enhance it with transitions, text, color correction, and other features.

CHAPTER EIGHT
WORKING WITH TITLES AND TEXT

Overview

We cannot talk about iMovie and its projects without emphasizing the need to work with titles and texts. In this chapter, you will learn how to work with titles and text and add them to your video.

How to add titles and text in iMovie

The process of preparing a video presentation or including narration in the film itself involves a certain level of skill with software packages that enable the addition of texts to a video or presentation. There will be a great number of cases in which you will wish to superimpose some text on top of a video. You may easily add a conventional title, a lower third subtitle, or scrolling credits to the movie by using iMovie on your Mac or iPhone. Both of these options are available to you. If you want to add text to films, iMovie is without a doubt one of the best software programs available.

To include text into your films using iMovie, you must first drag your media files to the timeline, and then proceed with the instructions that are listed below.

1. Simply displaying the text slides list requires you to click on the Text button.

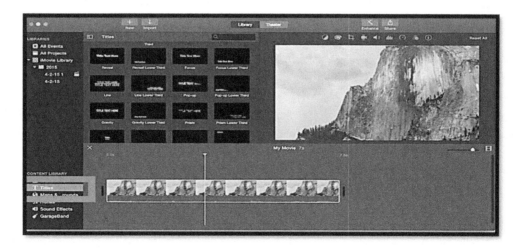

2. From this list, choose the text slide that corresponds to the project, and then drag the slide into the timeline for the project. In the slide, you have the option of either layering the slide or keeping it as a solo component.

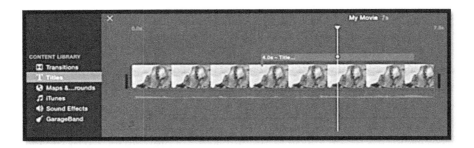

3. You can update the text by using the edit mode, which can be accessed by double-clicking inside the viewer interface. The font properties may be edited by clicking on the Show font's button, and then the changes can be saved by clicking on the Done button.

Changing the transition and placement properties may also be done by double-clicking on the project timeline, which will display the text inspector and allow you to make changes there.

How to create a title sequence or end credits

Adding End Credits to Your iMovie Projects

As a content writer, it is essential to have a solid understanding of the wide range of components that comprise video editing and production. Adding end credits to your iMovie films that appear like they were created by professionals is an important need. Before we get into the precise stages, let's first have a better understanding of the relevance of end credits in video productions. You can add a touch of professionalism to your films by including end credits, which not only provide recognition and credit to the people who were engaged in the production of the video. You may improve the overall quality of your production by including end credits, regardless of whether you are making a short film, a video for YouTube, or a presentation for a business.

Adding Centered End Credits in iMovie

A centered end credits feature in iMovie is going to be the first approach that we investigate using. Displaying names and titles after your film in a manner that is both clear and visually attractive is accomplished via the use of framed end credits.

Follow these procedures to add end credits that are centered:

1. Launch your iMovie project and go to the point in the timeline where you want the credits to be displayed after the movie.
2. Select the "**Centered**" option from the list of title styles that are accessible by clicking on the Titles button that is located in the iMovie toolbar.
3. The centered title should be dragged and dropped into your timeline after the primary video media has been added.

4. It is possible to enter the editing mode by double-clicking on the title clip.
5. Edit the text of the end credits that are centered, making any necessary adjustments to the font sizes, styles, and positions accordingly.
6. You can personalize the look of the text by picking several fonts, adding bold or highlighted options, and altering the colors.
7. Positioning the playhead and playing the timeline will allow you to see a preview of the closing credits.
8. Make adjustments to the length of the title clip to tailor the length of the end credits to your preferences.
9. You may want to think about adding background music or superimposing a background clip to increase the visual attractiveness.
10. Once you have saved and exported your iMovie project, the end credits that are centered will be included in the final video recording.

Giving your film a clean and professional appearance may be accomplished in a short amount of time and with no effort by using iMovie to add centered end credits. Through the completion of these stages, you will be able to create end credits that are visually appealing and that highlight your team as well as any relevant acknowledgments.

Adding Scrolling End Credits in iMovie

Adding end credits in iMovie with the use of scrolling credits is yet another option that is often used. You can show names, titles, and other information in a scrolling fashion after your project by using scrolling credits, which provide a visually dynamic approach to presenting the information.

These actions need to be taken to create scrolling end credits:

1. After opening your iMovie project, browse to the place where you want the credits to stop scrolling as they appear.
2. Choose the "**Scrolling Credits**" option from the list of title styles that are accessible by clicking on the Titles button that is located in the iMovie toolbar.
3. To add the scrolling credits title to your timeline, you will need to drag and drop it after the main video content.
4. To access the editing mode, double-click on the clip that contains the scrolling credits.
5. Make a copy of the text that you want to be included in the end credits, and then paste it into a rich text document editor like TextEdit.
6. Create the ideal scrolling effect by formatting the text in the document editor by modifying the fonts, widths, and line breaks to get the desired effect.
7. Take a copy of the text that has been prepared in the document editor.
8. You should go back to iMovie and then double-click on the text section of the clip that contains the scrolling credits.
9. Copy and paste the formatted text into the clip of the scrolling credits, making sure that it flows smoothly and remains within the space that has been defined.

10. Changing the length of the scrolling credits clip allows you to preview the credits as they scroll by playing the timeline and tweaking the pace of the credits as they advance.
11. If you want to improve the visual attractiveness of the scrolling credits, you may want to think about adding a backdrop or overlay.
12. After you have saved and exported your iMovie movie, the scrolling end credits will be included in the completion of the film.

The addition of scrolling end credits in iMovie makes it possible to create a depiction of the names and titles connected with your film that is both visually dynamic and visually interesting. You will be able to make scrolling end credits that will attract your viewers and give a professional touch to your films if you follow these guidelines.

Combining Different Types of End Credits

Creating a more thorough and visually attractive credit sequence in your iMovie productions may require you to mix several sorts of end credits. This is something you may want to consider doing in certain circumstances. For instance, you may begin with a succession of discrete titles for certain tasks or accomplishments, and then move into scrolling credits for a more comprehensive list.

The following procedures need to be taken to mix several styles of end credits:

1. iMovie allows you to either start a new project or open a current one.
2. Determine the sequence in which you would want the various kinds of end credits to appear in the final product.
3. The procedures that were mentioned before should be followed to add centered end credits or scrolling end credits according to the sequence that you decide to use.
4. Make adjustments to the fonts, colors, sizes, and layouts of each kind of end credit so that it conforms to your particular design preferences.
5. If you want to make sure that the transition between the various forms of end credits is smooth, you should play the timeline and preview the mix of end credits.
6. Think about adding extra creative elements into the credit sequence, such as animations, transitions, or background music, to increase the overall impact of the entire presentation.
7. After you have saved and exported your iMovie project, the combined end credits will be included in the finished film.

Adding a one-of-a-kind and personalized touch to your iMovie creations is possible with the combination of many kinds of end credits. To showcase certain persons or accomplishments while still preserving a professional and cohesive credit sequence, you may make use of this strategy.

Using Custom Graphics for End Credits

It is possible that you would want to consider using unique graphics to make your end credits more visually attractive and customized, even though iMovie gives a variety of tools and templates for making end credits. Through the use of picture editing software, you can create your graphics, which allows you to include distinctive components, emblems, or branding into your end credits.

Make sure you follow these procedures to use custom visuals for the end credits:

1. Image editing tools such as Adobe Photoshop or Canva can be used to either create or collect the personalized visuals that you want to include in your final credits.
2. Export the customized graphics as picture files in a suitable format, such as JPEG or PNG.
3. Launch your iMovie project and follow the on-screen instructions to get to the point where you want to add the custom graphics.
4. Import the custom graphics into your project by clicking on the button that is located in the toolbar of iMovie and selecting Photos and Audio.
5. Add the custom visuals to your timeline by dragging and dropping them after the main video content or before the end credits respectively.
6. Modify the look of the custom visuals as well as their location by scaling them, rotating them, or adding text overlays, at your discretion.
7. To provide a seamless transition from the custom visuals to the end credits, you should include any transitions or effects that are required.
8. To finish the credit sequence, you will need to follow the methods that were discussed before to add centered or scrolling end credits.
9. Check out the completed sequence and make sure that the custom visuals blend in well with the rest of the film.
10. After you have saved and exported your iMovie project, the graphics that you have created will be included in the finished video's end credits automatically.

The usage of custom graphics for end credits allows you to include parts of your own personal style, components of your business, or visual meaning into your iMovie productions. Simply by adhering to these instructions, you will be able to generate visually compelling end credits that will set your films apart from others and make an impression that will remain.

Creating End Credits as a Slideshow in Keynote

Although iMovie provides a variety of options for the construction of end credits, you may want to use Keynote since it provides a more sophisticated and adaptable method of making credits. Using Keynote, you can create intricate slideshows that include extensive text manipulation, transitions, and backdrops. After that, you can export these slideshows as films to be incorporated into your iMovie projects.

The following steps need to be taken to produce a slideshow of end credits using Keynote:

1. Launch Keynote on your Mac and a new presentation should be created.

2. Use Keynote's extensive features to choose an appropriate theme for your end credits slideshow or to develop a design that is unique to your presentation.
3. Create each slide according to your preferences, including text, pictures, animations, and background to properly display the credits that are pertinent to the presentation.
4. It is important to regulate the length of the presentation by setting the timing for each slide. This will ensure that there is ample time for visitors to read the credits.
5. You should make sure that the transitions between slides are seamless and visually attractive so that the slideshow flows smoothly from one slide to the next.
6. You should preview the full slideshow to confirm that the timing is correct, that it is readable, and that it is coherent overall.
7. The slideshow that you created in Keynote should be exported as a video file using the proper export option.
8. You will need to open your iMovie project and then import the Keynote movie that you exported into your timeline at the moment that you want it to terminate.
9. You may need to adjust the length of the Keynote video or its location to make it blend in smoothly with the larger video presentation.
10. After you have saved and exported your iMovie project, the slideshow that you created in Keynote will be used as the end credits in the finished film.

Using Keynote to create end credits in the form of a slideshow provides you with a wide range of customization choices and comprehensive flexibility, allowing you to present your credits in a visually attractive way. You can create elaborate presentations that boost the overall effect of your iMovie projects so long as you take use of the additional capabilities that Keynote offers.

Exploring Additional Options for Creative End Credits

Furthermore, in addition to the approaches that have been covered above, there are several additional possibilities and strategies that you may investigate to produce end credits in your iMovie movies that are both distinctive and entertaining.

Take the following options into consideration:

1. You should try out a variety of fonts, colors, and formatting choices to establish a style and theme that is consistent with the content of your film.
2. Add visual interest and dynamic effects to your end credits by using motion graphics, animations, or overlays throughout the presentation.
3. Use sound effects or background music to create an immersive experience during the segment of the movie that is dedicated to the end credits.
4. If you want to create complex end credits in iMovie, you should investigate the possibility of using third-party plugins or software solutions that provide specific functionality.
5. You may build unique end credits that are suited to your individual needs by working together with graphic designers or experienced video editors.

Create end credits that genuinely stand out and make a lasting impact on your viewers if you go beyond the standard approaches and explore extra choices beyond what is often done.

How to animate text in iMovie

Yes, it is possible to create the animation in iMovie; but, the procedure might be rather difficult for novices and those who are not technically savvy. For the same reason, we would be delighted to provide you with the most basic alternative to iMovie here. With that being said, let's begin with gaining an understanding of the benefits that come with animating text in iMovie or any other program. For example, let's discuss the miracles that can be accomplished by using animated text in the video clip that represents your company. The first advantage is that it simplifies the presentation of information that is otherwise difficult to understand. After that, the visually appealing appearance of dynamic text gives your project a more professional appearance than other projects. The enhanced involvement of the spectator may also be attributed to the animation of text in iMovie or animation created with other editors. Furthermore, it makes your information shareable across a larger audience base than it would **have been otherwise. In the following paragraphs, we will examine the actions that need to be taken to animate text in iMovie using Keynote animation.**

1. First, to continue with the iMovie text animation process in subsequent phases, you will need to download Keynote from the Mac store.
2. To add animated text to your iMovie movie, go to the project you want to add it to, move the playhead to the desired location, and then click the **Share button** to choose the Image. After that, it will provide this picture to you in the form of a JPEG, which you will need to import into Keynote. To do this, you will need to construct an animation (in this example, a lower-third animation) over the picture, remove the backdrop, and then export just the animation to iMovie as an overlay.
3. Before you delete the background of the slide, check to see that you have not chosen any of the objects on the slide. Proceed to the tab labeled "**No Fill**" in the Format menu.
4. To enter the Export window, choose **File > Export to > Movie** from the menu bar. After choosing the **Self-Playing option**, you will need to click the Cancel heading. The next step is to go to the **'Animate'** tab, as seen in the following image. Following the click on the Build Border tab shown below, you will now be able to see the Self-Playing parameters of the text animation. Once again, go to the File menu, then click Export, and then pick Custom in the resolution field. This will allow you to enter the exact resolution settings that will match in iMovie. After that, you will need to choose **Apple ProRes 4444** to export the animation with a translucent backdrop. Following that, to continue working with iMovie, you will need to choose the **Next > Save As > Export menu.**

5. To add an overlay to the project that was just finished, you will need to hover once more over the iMovie from Keynote and then drag the video file that you have just saved to the timeline of iMovie. To animate text in iMovie, you must first consider utilizing the Apple Keynote Presentation package. This is following the previous sentence. The explanation for this is that iMovie is not capable of producing animations of this type on its own.

Consequently, the procedures of installing Keynote, importing the files, and exporting them are a little bit more involved in this respect.

How to Add Typewriter Effect Titles to iMovie

You can add the typewriter effect to iMovie with the assistance of Keynote, even though the built-in library of title animations that comes with iMovie does not include the typewriter effect. Text is handled very well by the presentation program known as Keynote. Every aspect of the text, including the font, the background color, the size, and the hundreds of text effects, is entirely in your control. The ability to build a complicated type text effect and then utilize it in iMovie is at your disposal using Keynote.

Here are the steps:

1. First, start Keynote and go to its Wide Theme collection. Next, choose the blank white theme from the available options.
2. After making the necessary adjustments to the size of the slide and removing the sample text, go to the Color Fill option and use it to alter the background color of the slide to green.
3. You can write in your own words by clicking on the Text tool, and then you may alter them by changing the font, color, size, placement, and other aspects.
4. The next step is to pick the text, and then go to the animate button located in the upper right corner of the screen. After that, choose **Build In and Add an Effect,** and then select the **Typewriter effect** from the drop-down box.
5. After you have applied the Typewriter effect to your text and selected it, you will have the ability to modify several aspects, such as the duration and the direction. Ensure that the build order is checked here and that it begins after the transitions have been completed.
6. To examine the final output, you need to study the typewriter effect. Subsequently, go to the File menu and export the typewriter effect using the QuickTime video file format.
7. Now that you have the typewriter effect that you just made in Keynote, you can import it into iMovie and drag and drop it on the timeline so that it is immediately above the video clip that you want to apply the typewriter effect to. It is important to keep in mind that the Green/Blue Screen function of iMovie should be used to make the backdrop of the text overlay translucent.

Various text formatting options

To improve the quality of your video productions, iMovie 2024 provides you with several text formatting options.

The following are some of the majority of them:

1. **Font Styles**: iMovie allows you to choose from a wide range of font styles, ranging from the most fundamental to an assortment of more ornamental possibilities. You can choose a typeface that is appropriate for the atmosphere and tone of your film.
2. **Font Size**: Change the size of your text to make it more noticeable or less noticeable, based on your tastes and the style of your film. Font Size: Adjust the size of your text accordingly.
3. **Text Color**: Customize the color of your text to create visual contrast, compliment the background, or match your branding. Text color may be customized to fit your logo.
4. **Text Alignment:** A better composition and readability may be achieved by aligning your text to the left, center, or right of the screen according to your preference.
5. **Text Effects**: iMovie allows you to inject effects into your text, like fades, zooms, and rotations, to make it more dynamic and interesting to the viewer.
6. **Text Borders**: The addition of borders around your text may help it stand out from the background and increase its visibility. You can do this by adding borders around your text.
7. **Text Shadows**: If you want to give your text a sense of depth and dimension, you may apply shadows to it. This will make it easier to read against busy backgrounds.
8. **Text Animations:** iMovie has several different animation choices for text, which enables you to move it in and out of the frame, as well as add effects like bouncing or sliding.
9. **Text Transparency**: The transparency of your text can be adjusted so that it blends in perfectly with the background or so that you can create layered effects.
10. **Text Backgrounds**: If you want your text to be more apparent and visually beautiful, you may add background colors or shapes behind it.

How to Add Subtitles & Captions in iMovie

Captions and subtitles are very important, and you cannot disregard their significance if you are a content developer. Your material can reach a broader audience with the use of these visual aids, notably those of individuals who have issues with hearing or language. The question now is, how can you include them in your videos?

Is it possible for iMovie to put subtitles on films automatically?

Subtitles for films inside iMovie are not automatically generated by the program. That does not, however, imply that you should give up on the situation. There is a function in the program called Title that allows you to write in your subtitles and have them show over the video that you are watching. Although this method is arduous, it enables you to effortlessly add subtitles or captions to any movie that you choose.

Does iMovie have the capability to import an SRT file?

Unfortunately, the answer to this query is "**no**," since iMovie does not permit the direct importation of an SRT file into the program. Even if this is the case, you are still able to utilize the SRT file while you are making your subtitles. The text from the SRT file should be copied and pasted into the program to do this. If you choose the Title feature, you will be presented with a text box that accepts your input. Put the text in there by pasting it.

The proper steps:

While working with iMovie on a Mac, you can quickly add subtitles or captions to the material you are working with. When it comes to getting started with this one, you do not need any specialized expertise.

On the other hand, if the film is lengthy, it might serve as a brief exercise program for your fingertips. What you need to do to get started is as follows:

1. Launching iMovie on your Mac is a must for getting started with the project. If you are unable to locate the program on the dock, you should look in the Applications folder inside the finder window. To begin using iMovie, you must first double-click the icon.
2. The next step is for you to start a new project. After you have completed this step, you will be able to import the video to which you want to add subtitles. For the sake of getting things started, go to **Project**, then **Create New**, and finally **Movie**.

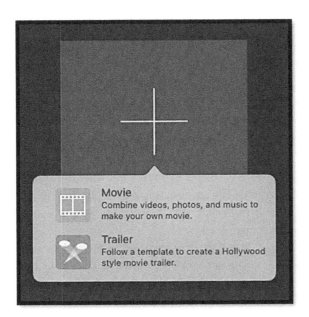

3. In the next step, you will need to import the video to which you want to add subtitles. To do this, choose the clips that you want to utilize by clicking on the Import Media button.
4. A video clip of yours will be shown in the box on the top left. After that, you will need to relocate it to the location of your choosing on the timeline. In this situation, you can make use of a simple drag-and-drop strategy. You can drag the media file to the timeline by clicking on it and dragging it down. The media file will have a thumbnail image.

5. iMovie makes it simple to add subtitles that have been hand-typed. To get started, you will need to click on the Titles button. After you have completed that step, you will be presented with a wide variety of styles, such as Split, Expand, Slide, and Focus. Pick the one that best fits the aesthetic of your brand image.

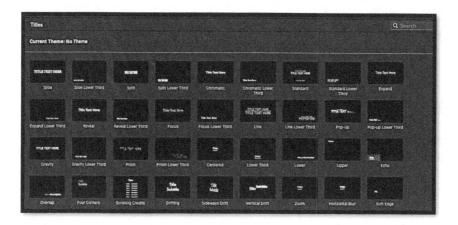

6. After you have decided on a style, you can then move the Title box to the timeline by dragging and dropping it. Choose the moment at which you would want the subtitles to start playing. A timestamp will be shown on each text box that you put in, and it will be placed above the video clip. It will be necessary for you to include numerous captions in your work. Make sure that your subtitles are typed straight into each of the Title boxes that you have added to the timeline when you have done so. If it is appropriate for your film, you may include a few distinct styles in it.
7. Once you have completed the process of typing out your subtitles and ensuring that they are correct, the following step is to make the subtitles seem more appealing. You are in luck since iMovie allows you to alter the text. For the Title box, click on one of the boxes. In the upper right corner of the screen, above the video, you will see a selection of fonts to choose from. Determine the dimensions, design, alignment, and color that are appropriate for your brand.

The procedure is finished when the video is saved, which is the last step. Simply choose the File option located at the very top of the screen. You should first choose the **Share option**, and then select **File** once again. In case a box displays, choose **Next**, give your video a name, and then select **Save**.

How to add subtitles or captions in iMovie on iPhone or iPad

Not everyone has a Mac. You may still add subtitles or captions to your movie even if you only have an iPhone or an iPad installed on your device.

Here are the actions you need to do to finish this task:

1. Open iMovie. Downloading this application from the App Store is something you can do if you do not already have it installed on your iOS device. After that, all you need to do is click the symbol that is shown on the screen of your phone, and the application will launch. A bar that reads "**Start New Project**" and has a few different options will be the first thing that you will see. Click the **Movie option** to proceed.

2. Next, you will need to import the video to which you want to add subtitles on your computer. You must make certain that you have a copy of the video clip stored on your iPad or iPhone device. The application will lead you to the videos that are stored on your iOS device after you have chosen the Movie option at the beginning of the process. By clicking on the one you want to use and then selecting the Create Movie button, you may choose the one you want to use.

3. After that, you will need to pick the **T button** located at the bottom of the screen and then click the media that is located in the timeline. You will see that a variety of Title styles will display under the timeline after you have completed that step. You should choose the one that best meets your requirements, and then move the timeline to the appropriate moment.

4. While the video is playing at the top of the screen, the text will show throughout the whole film. Simply pick Edit after clicking on it. When you are finished, you are free to write whatever text you like into the box. Whenever you push the **Play button**, it will be superimposed on top of the video clip at the moment that you previously selected.

5. Should you want to include several captions in your film, you may need to perform the technique described above many times. Alternatively, you have the option of selecting a different style for the Title.

6. The Done button can be found in the upper left-hand corner of the screen. Click it after you are satisfied with the captions you have created. Following that, you may save the file by clicking the Share button that is located at the bottom of the screen.

You have the option of transferring the movie to your pals using the AirDrop function or sharing it with them through WhatsApp or Messenger. Another option is to hit the **Save Video button**, which will cause the video to be saved to the iOS device that you are now using.

How to edit and stylize subtitles in iMovie

Now that you are familiar with the process of adding subtitles to iMovie, let's discuss the editing process for those subtitles. As soon as you have finished typing out your captions, you will have the opportunity to make changes to the text. There is a small variation in the procedure that occurs while you are using an iPhone, iPad, or Mac computer. Following the addition of subtitles to your film in iMovie on a Mac, you will then have the ability to alter the text. At the beginning of the procedure, you will have selected a style; nevertheless, there are more alternatives available to you.

This being said, to personalize the subtitles that appear on your video, you should follow the procedures that are listed below.

1. To begin, choose the **Title box** that you want to modify and click on it.
2. Second, move the pointer to the text options located in the upper right-hand corner of the screen.
3. The next step is to choose the font type by clicking the dropdown menu.
4. In the fourth step, pick the font size by using the dropdown menu.
5. Choosing the alignment you want for your captions.
6. Choose Bold (B), italic (I), or outline (O).
7. Select the color you want for your text by clicking on the color box.

What are the steps to modify subtitles in iMovie on an iPhone or iPad?

You can edit videos that you have made on your iPhone or iPad if you have used those devices instead. You could discover that the procedure is a little bit more complicated than you would anticipate it to be.

When you have finished adding the captions to your movie, you will need to proceed with the procedures that are listed below:

1. To begin, choose the Title box that you want to modify and click on it.
2. To choose the font style you want to use, select the **Aa button**.
3. The next step is to choose the font color by using the color circle button.
4. To see further choices that can be customized, go to the button and click on it.
- Both uppercase and lowercase fonts
- Text style
- Text shadows

You can make adjustments by using the toggle feature, or you can click on the alternatives that are shown above. After you have selected the text style that best meets your needs, you may proceed by clicking the **Done button**.

CHAPTER NINE
UNDERSTANDING AUDIO EDITING

Overview

Further editing means better quality in iMovie and there is no better way than understanding audio editing and using it to sync audio with video clips and removing background noise.

How to remove background noise and enhance audio clarity

Background noise can greatly diminish the quality of your videos. The presence of background noise in your videos can greatly impact the overall audio quality. By reducing this noise in iMovie, you can greatly enhance the sound captured on your iPhones or other iOS devices.

iMovie provides several built-in options that can assist you in dealing with background noise problems in your videos. There are three common approaches:

1. **Detaching Audio:** This method allows you to detach the audio track from your video clip, giving you the option to edit or replace the audio completely.
2. **Equalizer Tool (Mac Only):** For Mac users using iMovie, there is an equalizer tool available to fine-tune audio frequencies and potentially minimize any unwanted background noise.
3. **Muting the Audio:** Although it may not be suitable for every scenario, completely muting the audio can serve as a swift remedy when the background noise becomes overwhelming and there are no alternative audio options.

Considerations to Minimize Noise in Videos

The advancements in AI technology have made noise reduction incredibly smooth. However, certain precautions can be taken to reduce noise during recording. This section will cover the steps to reduce background noise in iMovie. These primary considerations can have a significant impact on noise levels:

Choose the ideal location

When it comes to recording audio or video, selecting the appropriate environment is crucial. While it's impossible to find a completely noise-free location, one can certainly make an effort to minimize noise. Quiet and serene locations with sparse populations and abundant natural surroundings are typically free from noise. Reserve a studio for video or audio recording, as it requires minimal effort. Their offerings include pre-arranged setups and space, complete with noise-canceling equipment.

Ensuring High-Quality Sound and Optimal Microphone Placement

A microphone is essential for creating high-quality audio and video content. A top-notch microphone excels in delivering exceptional sound. There are two microphone options available: an external microphone or a device-integrated microphone. In addition, the clarity of voice is determined by the position and settings of microphones. When the microphone is positioned closer to the speaker, it will produce a satisfactory sound for the speech.

Wind Protection and Interference

Outdoor shoots can be challenging due to the noise of wind. The audio quality not only suffers, but it also becomes a source of annoyance for the viewers. To minimize wind noise, consider using a windscreen or furry cover. For optimal performance, it is recommended to keep the recorder at a safe distance from electrical devices to minimize potential interference. These may include smartphones, laptops, and other similar devices.

Adjusting Audio and Gain Levels

It is crucial to monitor audio levels during recording to ensure better quality. Headphones can be used by creators to monitor audio levels and eliminate any unwanted background noises. Furthermore, we recommend adjusting the gain to ensure optimal clarity. The audio quality can be compromised by noise and other distortions when the gain value is high.

Proper Formats and Editing

Before commencing the recording process, it is essential to select an audio format of superior quality. WAV and FLAC are both popular and widely used high-quality formats. In addition, it is important to select editing software that includes noise-reduction capabilities. The software should ensure that the audio quality remains intact throughout the editing process. These tools also provide audio enhancement effects that can get the job done.

Simple Solution for Mac Users to Remove Background Noise: iMovie

iMovie is a fantastic built-in application specifically designed for macOS devices, allowing users to effortlessly create and edit videos. This software allows Mac users to easily edit their movies by adding music effects. Users can share their projects online or easily stream them on Apple TV using iMovie. iMovie offers powerful video and audio editing features, including the ability to reduce background noise. The software provides audio enhancement features to improve speech clarity and adjust audio equalization. The audio denoise function in iMovie seamlessly reduces background noise. The feature is built around its primary editing interface and is simple to use. Furthermore, it offers the ability to edit multiple audio formats, including ACC, MP3, and more.

Ways to Minimize Background Noise in iMovie

Are you a Mac user interested in learning how to remove background noise in iMovie? Follow this comprehensive step-by-step guide to learn all about noise reduction:

1. Begin by opening iMovie and selecting the **"Create New"** option. Then, import your media files. Next, use the drag-and-drop technique to easily add your media to the timeline.

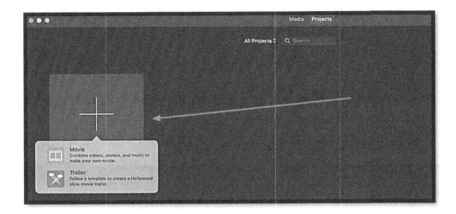

2. Proceed to the toolbar located at the top right and familiarize yourself with the available options. To begin editing, find and click on the **"Noise Reduction and Equalizer"** button.

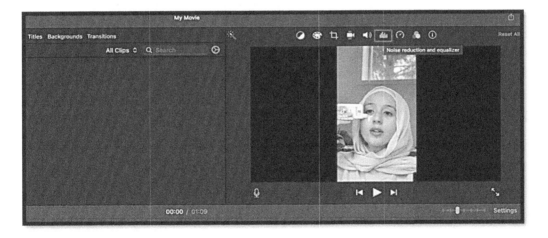

3. Find the **"Reduce background noise"** slider among the available options. Adjust the position of this slider to control the level of noise reduction.

4. Now, play your video to observe the outcomes and fine-tune the noise intensity. After you've achieved the desired outcome, you can either export your video or save it to iMovie.

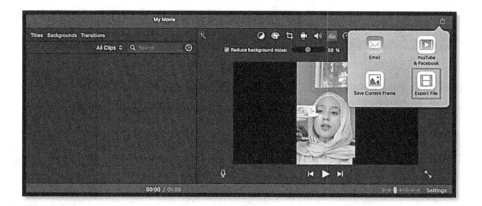

How to synchronize audio with video clips

It can be quite frustrating when you're working on a significant project, and the synchronization between the audio and video is not aligned. Fortunately, this issue can be resolved by implementing certain techniques with iMovie, which is an official Apple product.

Take a look at the steps below to discover the different methods for synchronizing audio and video using iMovie:

1. **Extract and Edit Audio**
You can easily detach the audio from a video in iMovie and make separate edits to it. If you're unfamiliar with how to execute that particular technique, follow the steps outlined below:
   - Open **iMovie** and click on File from the Menu bar. Now, choose **Import Media** and bring in the video you want to edit.

- After selecting the added clip, you can easily export the soundtrack by clicking on Detach Audio.
- Next, locate the **Audio file** on the timeline and choose the **Edit option**. Simply press Trim to Selection and make the necessary adjustments to match the video.
- Finally, complete the changes by selecting **File** and **Save**.

2. **Enhance Your Videos with External Audio using iMovie**

Here are the steps:

- Open the video you want to sync on iMovie.
- Drag the video and audio file to the iMovie timeline.

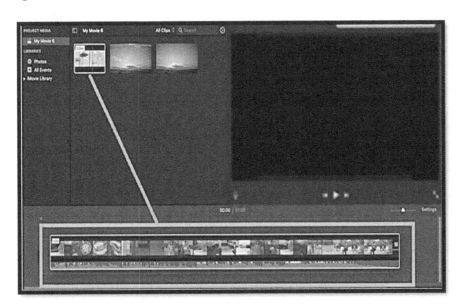

- After that, you can click on the **Video tab** and disable the **Speaker option** to remove the audio.

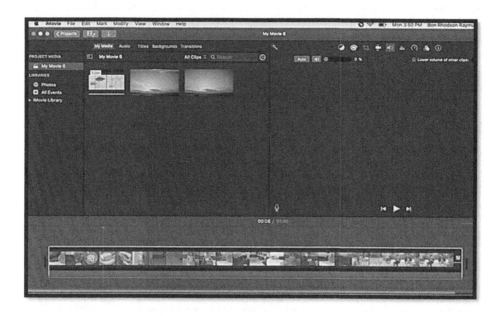

- Next, reinsert the audio file that was previously removed onto the timeline and ensure that it is properly synchronized with the video.

- To complete the process, select the **Share option** and proceed to **Export File** to save the video.

CHAPTER TEN
EXPORTING AND SHARING

Overview

What is the point of creating exciting iMovie projects without being able to share or export them to friends and family members? This chapter answers all your questions and gives you solutions to exporting and sharing your projects.

Email a movie, trailer, or clip in iMovie on Mac

You can easily include your movie, trailer, or clip in an email using Mail, the macOS email app. If a movie, trailer, or clip exceeds the maximum recommended email attachment size of 10 MB, a warning will appear when you try to share it in an email.

The steps:

1. Choose a movie, trailer, or clip from the browser in the iMovie app on your Mac.
2. Select **File**, then go to **Share** and click on **Email**.
3. In the dialog box that pops up, you can perform the following actions:
   - **Provide a title for the shared movie**: Simply click on the name at the top and enter a new name
   - Update the description of the shared movie by clicking on the **Description field** and entering new text.
   - **Set tags for the shared movie:** Enter tag names separated by commas in the Tags field.
   - **Adjust the resolution of the shared movie**: Select an option from the Resolution pop-up menu.
   - Note that it is possible to export a 4K clip or movie in its original resolution.
   - To expedite the export process, you can enable the "**Allow export segmentation**" option. This will help accelerate the export of projects that have duration of around 3 minutes or more. iMovie utilizes the processing power of multiple media engines to handle different segments of your video simultaneously.

Note that to perform export segmentation, you will need a Mac running macOS Sonoma or a later version, equipped with either Apple M1 Max, M1 Ultra, M2 Max, M2 Ultra, or M3 Max.

4. Click on the **Share button**.

There is a progress indicator located on the right side of the toolbar. Click on the progress indicator to view more information. Once the operation is complete, the indicator will no longer be visible.

Once the sharing process is finished, the movie will show up in a draft email with the project's title as the subject. A notification indicating that the share was successful also pops up.

How to share your iMovie projects on social platforms using a Mac

Prepare your movie for sharing on popular video-sharing websites.

Here are the steps:

1. Choose a movie, trailer, or clip from the browser in the iMovie app on your Mac.
2. Go to **File**, then select **Share**, and finally choose **Social Platforms**.
3. In the dialog that appears, you have the option to:

- Change the title of the shared movie by clicking on the name at the top and entering a new name.
- Update the description of the shared movie by clicking on the **Description field** and entering new text.
- **Add tags to the shared movie**: Click on the Tags field and enter tag names, separating them with commas.
- **Adjust the resolution of the shared movie:** Select an option from the Resolution pop-up menu.
- **Increase export speed with simultaneous processing**: Check the "**Allow export segmentation**" box to expedite exports of projects that are around 3 minutes or longer. iMovie sends segments of your video to available media engines for processing at the same time.

4. Select the "**Next**" option.
5. Choose a name for the output media file, and then select a location on your Mac or storage device to save the file. Finally, click **Save**.

The format of your project is perfect for sharing on social platforms. There is a progress indicator that can be found on the right side of the toolbar. Click on the progress indicator to view more information. Once the operation is complete, the indicator will disappear.

6. Make sure to carefully follow the instructions provided by the website or platform to successfully upload the file using a web browser like Safari.

How to export an image in iMovie on Mac

If you want to use a single frame of video from your movie with other apps, you have the option to export it as an image. The image is saved as a JPEG file.

Follow the steps below;

1. Open the **iMovie app** on your Mac and navigate to the clip or movie you want to export. Use the skim feature to quickly preview the content. Once you've found the desired frame, click on it.
2. Select **File**, then go to **Share** and click on **Image**.
3. In the dialog that appears, enter a name in the Save As field or keep the default name, which corresponds to the name of the movie, trailer, or clip.
4. Go to the location where you'd like to save the file, then click **Save**. Once the sharing process is finished, a notification will pop up indicating that the sharing was successful.

Export a movie, trailer, or clip as a file in iMovie on your Mac

Your movie can be exported as a file, allowing you to use it with other apps.

1. Choose a movie, trailer, or clip from the browser in the iMovie app on your Mac.
2. Select **File**, then go to **Share**, and finally choose **File**.
3. In the dialog box that pops up, you can perform the following actions:
- Change the title of the shared movie by clicking on the name at the top and entering a new name.
- Update the description of the shared movie by clicking on the Description field and entering new text.
- To set tags for the shared movie, simply click in the **Tags field** and enter the desired tag names, separating them with commas.
- Choose an option by clicking the Format pop-up menu to set the output format of the shared movie.
- You have the option to export either video and audio or solely audio.
- Adjust the resolution of the shared movie by selecting an option from the Resolution pop-up menu.

Note that it is possible to export a 4K clip or movie in its original resolution.
- Adjust the output quality of the shared movie by selecting an option from the Quality pop-up menu.

To adjust the output quality of the shared movie, simply follow these steps: click on the Quality pop-up menu, select Custom, and then use the slider to set the desired target bit rate. As the slider is adjusted, the file size estimate below the preview thumbnail is automatically updated.

- **Select a compression setting**: Open the Compress menu and choose the desired option.
- **Increase export speed with simultaneous processing**: Check the "**Allow export segmentation**" box to expedite exports of projects that are around 3 minutes or longer. iMovie sends segments of your video to available media engines for processing at the same time.
4. Select the "**Next**" option.

5. In the dialog box that pops up, you can either enter a name in the Save As field or keep the default name, which is the name of the movie, trailer, or clip.
6. Go to the location where you want to save the file, and click **Save**.

There is a progress indicator located on the right side of the toolbar. Click on the progress indicator to view additional information. Once the operation is complete, the indicator will disappear. Once the share process is finished, the movie will automatically open in QuickTime Player. A notification indicating that the share was successful also pops up.

If you're searching for iMovie Theater within iMovie on your Mac

Unfortunately, sharing to iMovie Theater is no longer supported. You can still view, share, and delete movies or trailers that you've shared with the Theater in previous iMovie versions. To enjoy uninterrupted access to your favorite movies and trailers across all your devices, it is recommended to import them into Photos and ensure that iCloud Photos is enabled. Once you have successfully imported all your movies and trailers into Photos, it is recommended to remove them from iMovie Theater.

Add movies or trailers in iMovie Theater to Photos

1. Open the iMovie app on your Mac and select **Window > Go to Theater**.
2. To share the movie or trailer, simply click the **More Options button** below and select **Copy to File**.
3. Go to the location where you wish to save the movie or trailer, and then select the **Save** option.
4. To import photos, go to the Photos app and select **File > Import**.
5. Go to the folder where you saved the movie or trailer, and select **Review for Import**.

For seamless access to your movie or trailer across all your devices, it's important to have iCloud Photos enabled. To do this, go to **Photos > Settings**, click on **iCloud**, and select **iCloud Photos**.

Remove a movie or trailer from iMovie Theater

If you decide to delete a movie or trailer in the Theater, you have the option to remove it solely from iCloud or from iCloud, your Mac, and all of your devices. The source project and related media have not been deleted, so you can make edits to the project.

Follow the steps below:

1. Open the iMovie app on your Mac and select **Window > Go to Theater**.
2. To delete a movie or trailer, simply click the **More Options button** located under the desired video, and then select **Delete**.

3. **Choose one of the following options:**
- **Delete from iCloud**: The movie or trailer will still be accessible on your Mac, but it will be removed from iCloud.
- **Delete Everywhere**: The movie or trailer is eliminated from iCloud, your Mac, and all of your iOS and iPad devices.

Using AirDrop with iMovie

1. **Exporting the iMovie Project**: First, you'll want to export your iMovie project to a format that is compatible with your needs. Here's how you can do this:
- Open your iMovie project.
- Access the "**File**" menu located at the top-left corner of the screen.
- Choose "**Share**" from the dropdown menu.
- Make sure to select the export option that best suits your requirements. As an illustration, you have the option to export to file formats such as MP4 or MOV.
2. Use AirDrop to easily share your iMovie project with another Apple device after exporting it to a compatible format. Here is the step-by-step process:
- Ensure that AirDrop is enabled on both your Mac and the iOS device (iPhone, iPad) that will be receiving the file.
- Find the exported iMovie project file on your Mac.
- To access the context menu, simply right-click (or Control-click) on the file.
- Choose "**Share**" from the menu and then select "**AirDrop**."
- A list of nearby devices that support AirDrop will be displayed. Choose the device you wish to share the file with.
- Accept the AirDrop request on the receiving device to receive the file.
3. If you've shared the iMovie project with an iOS device, you may need to import it into iMovie on that device. Here is a step-by-step guide to help you accomplish this:
- Open the **Files app** on your iOS device.
- Go to the location where the iMovie project file was saved.
- Open the project file by tapping on it.
- If prompted, select the option to open the file in iMovie.
- After importing the project into iMovie on your iOS device, you can edit or view it according to your requirements.

CHAPTER ELEVEN
OVERLAYS AND KEYFRAMING

Overview

Chapter eleven discusses overlays and keyframing in iMovie. Here, you will learn what overlay is and how to carry out some functions including using cutaways to hide jump cuts, how to use transitions, and much more.

Understanding overlays in iMovie

iMovie Video Overlay Options

Before we get into the process of how to overlay films in iMovie to create picture-in-picture effects, let's take a short look at the various choices available for video overlays in iMovie. There **are four different overlay options available in iMovie, which is one of the many wonderful features made available by iMovie.**

- **Cutaway**: One of the default overlay options in iMovie is called Cutaway. If you choose the cutaway method to overlay your video, the project will transition to the footage that is located above the original track at certain points in the timeline. After the overlay video, your project will return to the primary clip itself.
- **Green/Blue Screen**: When you use the Green/Blue Screen option to overlay your video on the main clip, the video clip will appear with the green-screen or blue-screen sections of the clip removed. The remaining parts of the clip will be overlaid on the main clip in the timeline while the green-screen or blue-screen parts of the clip are deleted.
- **Split Screen**: The Split Screen overlay gives you the ability to show two films or pictures next to one other. In this section, you also can change the orientation of the clips so that one clip floats over the other.
- **Picture in Picture:** The Picture in Picture option enables you to add a picture or video to a tiny portion of the screen. The clip will be displayed in a smaller window, overlaid on the main clip in the timeline. Picture in Picture is a feature that is available in the timeline.

Why Should You Make a Video Overlay?

The creation of a video overlay is something that you should think about doing for several different reasons. This includes the following:

Enhancing the level of viewer engagement

The promotion of increased viewer engagement is one of the most prominent motivations for the creation of a video overlay. When you create a video overlay, you can add interactive features such as clickable buttons, hotspots, or links right on top of the video content. This helps to raise the level of viewer engagement by providing them with more methods to interact with and explore the video.

Additional context

The creation of an overlay is one of the most successful methods to accomplish the goal of providing more contexts in your movies, and it is one of the finest ways to accomplish this goal. Because it enables you to show supplemental information, subtitles, or images that provide more depth to your video material, video overlay may assist your viewers in better comprehending the message or content that is being delivered to them.

Enhance the branding and messaging

Making improvements to your message and identity is yet another reason why you could find it necessary to build a video overlay. Reiterating your brand identity and ensuring that your most important messages are sent to viewers can be accomplished by superimposing text, logos, or other branded components on top of the video.

Access Easy Content Updates

It is much simpler to update or refresh certain aspects of a video, such as text or images, with the use of video overlays, since this eliminates the need to re-shoot or re-edit the whole video presentation. If you want to maintain your information up-to-date and relevant without having to put in a lot of effort, this is an excellent method.

Create cinematic effects

You can improve the overall aesthetic of your movie by superimposing visual effects such as film grain, light leaks, or other creative filters. This will make your video seem more polished and will give it a cinematic appearance and feel.

How to Overlay Videos in iMovie for Picture-in-Picture Effects and Other Additional Features

If you want to keep your audience interested in your film, adding a video over a video is a terrific idea.

Follow the steps to overlay videos in iMovie on Mac:

1. When you open your iMovie project on your Mac, check to see that all of your films have been imported so that you may work with them.
2. You will need to set the playhead in the location where you want to insert the video overlay, and then you will need to drag and drop the second video into the timeline. After that, you will have successfully inserted the video overlay.

3. You should now have two films on the timeline. To change the settings for the video overlay, pick the video overlay, go to the iMovie toolbar at the top of the screen, and locate the Video Overlay Settings option.

4. After you have clicked the overlay option, you will see the various sorts of overlays along with a little download arrow. Simply click the download arrow and choose from a variety of different ways to place the video. In addition to the picture-in-picture mode, you also have the option of setting up positions such as cutaways, split-screen, green/blue screens, and more.

5. At this point, you can make any necessary adjustments to the overlay that is shown on your screen. After you have finished editing the film and working on overlays in the iMovie video, you will be able to start exporting it on your Mac. Simply go to the **File Menu**, choose **Share**, and then select **File**. From there, select the format, resolution, and quality that you want to use to save the video.

How to use cutaways to hide jump cuts

What is a Jump Cut?

Describe a Jump Cut as a shot that has been cut up into many portions and the most effective way to apply this technique is to visually represent the passage of time. In contrast to the majority of projects, which try to provide a seamless experience, Jump Cuts does the exact opposite and reveals the breaks, which goes against the notion of continuity. This decision, if implemented well, has the potential to have a tremendous influence on the experience that the viewer has, but it is relatively simple to execute incorrectly. Following the clarification of the term, we will now go on to the questions that will address where and how a Jump Cut may be used by an individual.

Where can you use a Jump Cut, and how can you use it?

If you want to include Jump Cuts in a video production, the following are examples of situations in which you should use them:

1. You wish to display a montage of different things, such as, for instance, food, beverages, accommodation, and so on.
2. If you want to add new characters, the transition from one to the next via the use of abrupt cuts should not provide too much of a challenge.
3. Increasing the suspense in a scene is something you want to do, and one way to do it is by progressively zooming in on an object with each cut.
4. To demonstrate the passage of time, alter the subject or the setting of a photograph to achieve this effect.

You should be aware that keyframing, which is an essential tool for video editing, often contributes to the creation of transitions that are more seamless and generate effects that are quite different from those that may be produced by a Jump Cut. The following is a list of the actions that need to be taken to produce a Jump Cut in iMovie, now that we have understood the fundamentals of a Jump Cut.

How to make a Jump Cut in iMovie

Following the steps that are given below is something you may begin doing once you have iMovie open and ready to go.

1. To begin a new long-format project, the first step is to choose the **Movie option**.

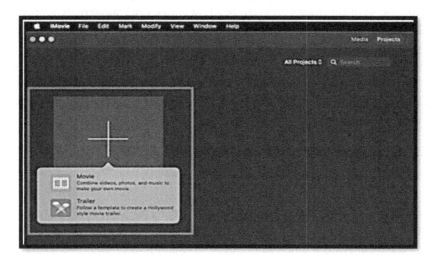

2. Import your video clip and then drop it into the Timeline.

3. Press the **Command key** and the B key simultaneously to split your video clip, and then make a second clip at the point where you want the first clip to end. It is important to note that the context menu also allows you to make a split. To activate the Trackpad, either right-click on it or touch it with two fingers.

4. Delete any clips that aren't necessary. A gap will be created as a result, which you will be able to fill up.

If you need to produce a jump cut, it is also recommended that you separate the audio from your video clip. This will assist you in recognizing the blank audio parts, which will lead to the possibility of making a better cut that will have a more significant impact.

How to create opacity effects

The following is a guide that will walk you through the process of creating opacity effects in iMovie 2024. This will allow you to add visual appeal to your films.

Follow the steps below:

1. Start iMovie and import the video clip you wish to work with into your project. This is the first step in the process of importing your media.
2. Drag your video clip into the timeline in the sequence that you want it to appear. This is the second step in the process of placing clips on the timeline.
3. To choose the clip you wish to modify, click on it. You will know that it has been chosen when it is highlighted in yellow.
4. To access the Clip Adjustments, click on the "**Adjust**" button that is located in the toolbar that is located above the viewer. This button seems to have three sliders. When you do this, the Adjustments pane will appear.
5. You can alter the opacity of your clip by using the Adjustments window, which has many different options for doing so. Track down the slider for the opacity. Drag the slider to the left to reduce the opacity, or to the right to raise it. This will allow you to adjust the opacity. You will be able to see the impact in real-time in the viewer as you make adjustments.
6. The use of keyframes is optional, although it is possible to utilize them if you want to produce a progressive shift in opacity with time. Choose the clock icon that is located next to the slider for the opacity. Because of this, keyframes will be able to have opacity. Move the playhead to the place in the clip where you want the opacity change to begin, and then click the "**Add Keyframe**" button that looks like a diamond. The opacity slider should be adjusted after the playhead has been moved to the location where you wish the opacity adjustment to finish. When you switch between keyframes, iMovie will automatically produce a seamless transition.
7. After you have reached a point where you are content with the opacity effect, you should do a preview of your adjustments by playing through your video.
8. When you are satisfied with the project you have created, pick "**Share**" from the "**File**" menu to export your video.

How to add fade transitions to overlays

The following procedures need to be taken to create fade transitions to overlays in iMovie 2024:

1. Launch iMovie and open the project where you want to add fade transitions to overlays. This includes opening the project where you want to add the transitions.
2. To add an overlay, just drag the overlay clip into the timeline and place it directly above the clip that you want it to overlay.
3. This will allow you to pick the overlay by clicking on the overlay clip that is located in the timeline.
4. Double-clicking on the overlay clip will reveal the Clip options window, which will allow you to access the overlay options.
5. Adjust the length of the overlay: If an adjustment is required, make sure that the duration of the overlay clip is the same as the duration of the clip that it is superimposing.

6. To add a transition, be sure to click on the "**Transitions**" button located in the toolbar. This button is shaped like two squares that overlap each other.
7. From the list of transition choices, choose a fade transition to use. Several choices, such as crossfade, fade to black, and others, are available for your selection.
8. Apply the transition by dragging the fade transition that you have selected and dropping it in the timeline between the overlay clip and the clip that overlay as a transition.
9. If necessary, make adjustments to the duration of the transition by dragging its edges in the timeline.
10. To get a preview of the fade transition between the overlay clip and the underlying clip, play through your project and see how it appears.
11. If any modifications are required, make any necessary edits to the overlay clip or the transition to create the look that you want.
12. You should save your project after you have determined that the fade transitions on your overlays are complete and satisfactory.

How to use zoom and swap transitions with PiP

Video is one of the most powerful tools that we have at our disposal in today's fast-paced digital world, where storytelling has grown to cover a broad variety of media because of the proliferation of digital technology. As a result of the development of user-friendly editing software like iMovie 2024, the process of producing movies that have a professional appearance is now more accessible than it has ever been. The capability of iMovie to include zoom and swap transitions with Picture-in-Picture (PiP) effects stands out as a dynamic method to engage viewers and enrich the visual story of your projects. This is just one of the many capabilities that iMovie has to offer.

Learn the Differences between Zoom and Swap Transitions

It is crucial to have a solid understanding of the relevance of zoom and swap transitions in iMovie 2024 before delving into the complexities of using them.

This is because these transitions may significantly improve the quality of your narrative.

- **Zoom Transitions:** Creating a smooth transition effect between two clips is accomplished via the use of zoom transitions, which require dynamically zooming in or out of a frame on each side of the transition. Your films will have more fluidity and energy as a result of this method, which seamlessly transitions the viewer's attention from one scene to the next in a visually fascinating way.
- **Swap Transitions**: Swap transitions, on the other hand, involve switching around one clip for another in a seamless manner while still maintaining the same frame. This method makes it possible to juxtapose a variety of pictures or points of view, which makes narrative development and visual storytelling much easier to do.

Understanding How to Begin Using iMovie 2024

The following simple steps are that entire are required to get started with using the power of zoom and switch transitions with PiP in iMovie 2024:

1. On your Mac device, launch iMovie 2024 and either begin a new project or open a current one in which you want to add these transitions.
2. To begin working on your iMovie project, take the video clips that you wish to use and import them. Make sure that the clips are arranged in the order that you need them to appear in the final video that you are creating.
3. To arrange your clips, just drag & drop them into the timeline in the order that you want them to appear. This stage establishes the groundwork for the subsequent steps, which include implementing transitions between zoom and swap.

Applying Zoom Transitions

Right now, let's have a look at how to use zoom transitions between the several video clips you have:

1. To choose the transition point, position the playhead at the point where you want the zoom transition to take place. This will represent the moment at which the transition between the two clips will take place.
2. Select the "**Transitions**" button that is situated above the timeline to access the available transition options. By performing this operation, a menu that displays a variety of transition effects will popup.
3. Select the Zoom Transition option from the transition menu. The "**Zoom**" option is the right one. iMovie has several possibilities for zoom transitions, including zoom in, zoom out, and diagonal zoom, among others. Whichever one works best with the overall style of your video should be selected.
4. Once you have selected the zoom transition that you want to use, you will need to drag & drop it into the transition point on the timeline that is located between the two clips. The transition effect will be applied automatically by iMovie, which will zoom down from one clip to the next in a smooth manner.

Incorporating Swap Transitions

Let's move on to the next step, which is to discuss the process of implementing swap transitions into your project:

1. Like zoom transitions, place the playhead at the transition point between two clips in which you want to apply the swap effect.
2. To access the transition options, go to the "**Transitions**" menu and pick the "**Swap**" transition option.

3. iMovie provides several different swap transition variants, such as horizontal swap, vertical swap, and diagonal swap. Select the switch effect that most closely corresponds to the creative concept you have in mind.
4. The transition can be applied by dragging and dropping the swap transition that has been chosen onto the transition point on the timeline that is located between the two clips. It is possible to create a transition effect that is visually interesting by using iMovie, which will effortlessly switch one clip for another.

Improvements to Transitions Through the Use of Picture-in-Picture (PiP) Effects

You have the option of incorporating Picture-in-Picture (PiP) effects into your project to further enhance the transitions that you have created. You can add depth and complexity to your transitions by using PiP, which enables you to superimpose one video clip on top of another.

To include PiP effects with zoom and switch transitions, the following steps should be taken:

1. To produce the PiP effect, select the video clip that you want to superimpose on top of another clip.
2. Using the settings that appear on the screen, you can adjust the size and position of the PiP clip to your liking. To get the desired visual impact, you can make adjustments to the size, location, and orientation of the PiP clip.
3. The next step is to add a transition between the PiP clip and the underlying clip on the timeline. Once you have positioned the PiP clip, you can apply a zoom or swap transition between the two clips. Following this phase, the PiP effect will be effortlessly integrated into your transition, which will enhance both the visual continuity and the narrative.
4. Preview the transition with the PiP effect applied, and then make any required tweaks to ensure that the transition is smooth and consistent. To acquire the best possible outcomes, you can perform adjustments to the timing, length, and positioning of the PiP clip.

How to use transition effects

The user-friendly video editing program developed by Apple, iMovie, gives producers the ability to weave their narrative using a wide variety of transition effects available to them. These transition effects will help you take your films to a more professional level, regardless of whether you are just starting as an editor or have years of expertise under your belt.

Gaining an Understanding of Transition Effects

Transition effects act as a bridge between two clips, allowing for a seamless transition from one scene to the next. The effects may range from straightforward fades to more dynamic effects such as wipes and slides. They are available in a variety of formats. iMovie 2024 makes it easy for users to access and apply these effects, which enables them to simply improve their films with transitions that are of a professional standard. The first step in introducing transition effects into your project is to launch iMovie and browse the timeline view. Once you have done this, you will be able to access transition effects. When you wish to place a transition between two clips, position the playhead such that it is between the clips. In the next step, choose the **"Transitions"** tab that is situated above the timeline. There are a wide variety of transition effects available in iMovie, which are arranged into a variety of styles. Some examples of these styles include dissolve, slide, fade, and others. Once you have selected a transition effect, all you need to do is drag it into the timeline in the middle of the two segments. iMovie gives you a visual preview of the transition, which enables you to examine it and alter the length of the transition according to your preferences. Furthermore, you can personalize the transition by clicking on it and gaining access to the **"Inspector"** panel. This panel allows you to fine-tune aspects such as the length, direction, and alignment of the transition.

To make successful use of transitions, it is essential to choose a suitable effect that compliments the atmosphere and story of your film. This is the secret to good transition utilization. To communicate a feeling of peacefulness or the passage of time, for example, soft fades are an effective technique. Dynamic effects, such as slides and flips, are also useful for adding energy and excitement to sequences that are moving at a rapid speed. Experimenting with a variety of transitions may assist you in locating the transition that is the most suitable for your project. Although transition effects have the potential to improve the quality of your movie, using them excessively or picking effects that are not suitable might cause the watching experience to be disrupted. It is recommended that you make use of strategies such as match cuts to achieve seamless transitions. Match cuts are a technique that involves features in succeeding clips mirroring or complementing each other to create a smooth transition without attracting attention to the effect itself. If you want to further improve the flow of your movie, you may do so by employing natural transitions such as camera moves or scene changes.

Increasing the Impact of Transitions with Sound

In addition to the use of visual effects, the incorporation of sound effects or ambient sounds may increase the impact of your transitions more effectively. The iMovie program comes with a collection of pre-installed sound effects; however, you also have the option to add your audio files to personalize the project's aural experience. It is possible to provide your audience with a viewing experience that is consistent and immersive by synchronizing the time of transitions with the sound effects.

Guidelines for sophisticated Transitions

iMovie 2024 has tools like green screen effects and keyframing, which let users have more creative control over transition animations. These capabilities are designed for consumers who are looking for more sophisticated transition approaches. Green screen effects give you the ability to smoothly overlay clips, and keyframing gives you the ability to create bespoke animations and motions inside your transitions, which gives your films a more professional appearance. When you have finished perfecting your transitions and finishing the editing process, it is time to export your project so that you may share your masterpiece with the rest of the world on the internet. There are several different export choices available in iMovie, such as saving to your smartphone, exporting in high-quality formats for professional usage, and direct sharing to social networking networks. Make sure that your video looks its best wherever it is seen by selecting the export parameters that are most appropriate for the audience you wish to reach and the distribution channel you intend to use.

How to use green and blue screen effects

It is crucial to make sure that you have a solid understanding of the fundamental concepts before going into the complexities of green and blue screen effects. During the shooting process, green screens and blue screens are used as backgrounds. This gives editors the ability to change the background with other material or video during the post-production phase.

How to Select the Appropriate Background

The selection of a suitable backdrop is fundamental to the achievement of a good green screen or blue screen effect. It is important to take into consideration the lighting, color scheme, and overall atmosphere of your scene while selecting a background. If your subject is positioned against a vivid green screen, for instance, you should choose a background that compliments rather than competes with the subject on the screen.

Placing Your Shot in Position

When filming, an appropriate setup is the first step in achieving the best results. To prevent shadows and inconsistencies, you should make sure that the lighting on your green or blue screen is uniform. In addition, ensure that your subject is positioned at an acceptable distance from the screen to avoid color leakage, which occurs when the color of the backdrop reflects onto the subject.

Bringing footage into iMovie for editing

Importing your film into iMovie is the next step to do once you have finished recording it. Start the application and either start a new project or open an existing one. Open an existing project. You can import your video by going to the location of your files and choosing **"File" > "Import Media"** from the menu. The editing process may begin by dragging and dropping the clips into the timeline.

Using the Green Screen or the Blue Screen Effect

At this point, the green or blue screen effect should be applied to the film that is currently on the timeline. The "**Video Overlay Settings**" button should be clicked once the clip that contains your topic has been selected and placed against the green or blue screen. From the selection that drops down, choose "**Green/Blue Screen.**"

An Adjustment to the Settings

To fine-tune your green or blue screen effect, iMovie provides several different options. Make adjustments to the strength of the effect by using the "**Strength**" slider. This will ensure that the subject and the backdrop merge without any noticeable gaps. Furthermore, make use of the "**Edge Detection**" slider to fine-tune the edges of your subject, therefore minimizing any roughness or artifacts that may be present.

Adding Effects and Backgrounds to the Scene

After you have created the green screen or blue screen effect, it is time to replace the backdrop with the video or images of your choosing. Import the backdrop you want to use into iMovie, then drag it into the timeline and put it below the clip that has the green or blue screen effect applied to it. Make adjustments to the time and length of the backdrop to achieve flawless synchronization with your film.

Improving Your Content and Structure

To improve the composition of your scene as a whole, you may want to think about adding some extra effects and tweaks. The lighting and color temperature of your subject should be matched with the background, therefore experiment with different color-correcting tools to achieve this. Applying transitions, filters, and overlays to your project can help you achieve a greater sense of depth and visual intrigue.

Refinement and a Preview of the Work

Spend some time perfecting your green or blue screen effect as well as the general composition of your project before you end up putting the finishing touches on it. You should do a comprehensive preview of your project to guarantee that the transition between the topic and the background is smooth and believable. It is required to make any necessary modifications to reach the objective.

Exporting your Project

It is time to export your project after you have reached a point where you are content with your creation. Proceed to the "**File**" menu and pick "**Share**" > "**File.**" From there, select the export parameters that you want to use, which may include options for resolution, format, and compression respectively. Before beginning the process of exporting your file, you must first click "**Save**" and then "**Next**" to pick the location for your exported file.

CHAPTER TWELVE
COLLABORATIVE EDITING WITH ICLOUD

Overview

Chapter twelve focuses on how users can use collaborative editing with iCloud in iMovie. You will be able to set up iCloud for collaborative editing and share collaborative projects using iMovie.

How to set up iCloud for collaborative editing

When it comes to creative undertakings like video editing, teamwork is particularly important in this day and age of digital technology. It is now easier than ever before to produce spectacular films thanks to the development of technology and the availability of programs such as iMovie. And now, with the integration of iCloud, working together on projects in iMovie has become even more streamlined and effective.

Understanding iCloud Collaboration in iMovie 2024

Before entering into the process of setting up iMovie 2024, it is vital to have a solid understanding of how the iCloud collaboration feature works. You can keep your iMovie projects safely and securely in the cloud with the help of iCloud, which enables you to view them from any device that is linked to those projects. This makes it possible for numerous people to collaborate on the same project at the same time, regardless of where they are located. This makes collaboration simpler and more flexible than it has ever been before.

The steps:

1. The first thing that needs to be done is to make sure that iCloud Drive is activated on all of the devices that will be used for collaborative editing. To do this, go to the Settings menu on your iOS device or the System Preferences menu on your Mac. From there, click iCloud and check to see whether iCloud Drive is enabled.
2. For the next step, you will need to enable iCloud for iMovie in particular. Open iMovie on your device, then go to **Preferences > iCloud** and tick the box next to "**Enable iCloud**." This will enable iCloud to be used. Your projects will be able to be synchronized across all of the devices that are linked to your iCloud account as a result of this.
3. Now that iCloud has been enabled, you can develop a new project in iMovie or open an existing one. After you have completed this step, your project will be saved to iCloud automatically, which will allow you to access it from any device that is signed in with the same iCloud account.
4. To work together on a project, you will need to invite other users to enlist their participation. Start by selecting the Collaborate option located in the toolbar of iMovie. After that, you will need to input the email addresses of the individuals you want to invite.

They will be sent an offer to participate in the project using iCloud, and after they accept the request, they will be able to access and edit the project alongside you.

5. If you have enabled iCloud collaboration, you and your collaborators will be able to work on the project concurrently and in real-time. Every modification made by a single user will be automatically synchronized to all of the other users' devices, enabling seamless collaboration regardless of the location of the users.

6. It is necessary to assess the changes that are being made to the project frequently and offer feedback to the people who are in collaboration with you. You can post comments directly on certain clips or portions of the project thanks to the built-in commenting tool that is included in iMovie. This feature makes this process quite simple.

7. Once the editing process is over, save the completed file to iCloud so that it can be accessed by all of the people who worked on it. You will then be able to simply share the project with other people by either emailing them a link to it or exporting it to a file format of your choosing inside that platform.

The Most Effective Methods for Working Together on Editing in iMovie

They include the following:

- **Communicate Clarity:** The ability to communicate effectively is essential to the success of any cooperation. It is imperative that you maintain open lines of communication with your partners and that you communicate any modifications or suggestions openly and honestly.

- **Delegate duties and Responsibilities**: To simplify the editing process, it is important to delegate duties and responsibilities to each contributor based on their respective areas of knowledge and abilities. This will assist in guaranteeing that everyone is aware of what they are accountable for and that they can collaborate to achieve a shared objective effectively.

- **Save and back up your projects regularly:** Even though iCloud offers powerful synchronization and backup features, it is always a good idea to save and back up your projects on your local device as well. This not only provides an additional degree of protection but also guarantees that you will not lose any work if there are any technical difficulties or connection challenges.

- **Show respect for version control:** When numerous users are working on the same project, it is essential to show respect for version control and to prevent overwriting each other's work. If you want to prevent disagreements and make sure that everyone is working on the most recent version of the project, you should make sure that any modifications or updates to the project are communicated to your collaborators.

How to collaborate communication channels

It is necessary to have a solid understanding of the reasons why cooperation is of the utmost importance in video creation before delving into the technical components. Not only can collaborative efforts improve workflow efficiency, but they also encourage creative thinking and new product development. Teams can handle difficult tasks with more ease and generate content that is richer and more interesting when they combine the varied skill sets and views contained among their members. The key to successful cooperation is effective communication, which ensures that every member of the team is kept informed, aligned, and given the authority to offer their best work.

When it comes to iMovie, integrating communication channels

1. **Determining the Roles and Objectives That Are Appropriate**

The first step is to establish crystal-clear project goals and delegate precise responsibilities to every member of the team. Whether it's editing, scripting, or offering comments, having a clear understanding of tasks helps reduce misunderstanding and encourages responsibility. When outlining tasks, establishing deadlines, and monitoring progress, it is helpful to make use of project management software such as Trello or Asana.

2. Taking Advantage of the Built-in Features of iMovie

iMovie comes with several built-in features that make it easier to work together, including:

- **Comments and Annotations**: Instruct members of the team to provide comments and annotations immediately inside the timeline of iMovie. Consequently, this makes it possible to provide contextual feedback, which improves communication and reduces the need for various communication platforms.
- **Sharing and Collaboration:** By using the sharing features of iMovie, you can collaborate in real-time with other users. Every member of the team can access the same project at the same time, which enables seamless collaboration regardless of where they are physically located.

3. **Including Channels of Communication Open to the Outside World**

Although iMovie has extensive in-app collaboration tools, the use of external communication channels may further improve teamwork:

- **Messaging Platforms:** Communication is centered on platforms such as Slack and Microsoft Teams, which act as centers for communication. Set up specific channels for having conversations about the project, exchanging files, and providing rapid updates.
- **Video Conferencing**: To discuss project milestones, address issues, and come up with ideas, you should schedule frequent video conferences using Zoom or Google Meet. Interactions that take place in person may help strengthen ties between members of a team, which in turn can build a feeling of camaraderie and encourage cooperation.

4. **Establishing Different Protocols for Communication**

To speed up interactions and reduce the likelihood of misunderstandings, clear communication standards should be established:

- **Designated Communication Times**: Determine particular time slots for communication, making certain that members of the team have periods that are committed to working together without distractions coming in.
- **Anticipated Levels of Response**: It is important to establish expectations about the response times for emails and texts. Providing prompt replies helps to cultivate a culture of responsiveness and responsibility, which in turn helps to keep projects on budget.
- **Providing Evidence of Decisions:** By recording significant choices and conversations in a single spot, you can ensure that you do not lose sight of them. Even if they were unable to take part in the talk directly, this means that everyone will continue to be informed and in agreement with the situation.

How to share collaborative projects

In iMovie 2024, the process of sharing collaborative projects has grown more streamlined and effective, making it possible for groups to work together on creative undertakings without any difficulty. iMovie has a wide range of capabilities that facilitate collaboration and sharing, making it suitable for a variety of projects, including personal films, business presentations, and school projects.

Understanding Collaborative Projects in iMovie 2024

It is possible for numerous people to concurrently work on the same project in iMovie 2024 because of the collaborative projects feature. This function is very helpful for groups of people who are working remotely together or for individuals who are working together on creative projects. iMovie can expedite the process of collaboration by providing real-time synchronization and cloud-based storage. This will ensure that everyone is on the same page during the whole process.

Getting Started

The following actions need to be taken to get a collaborative project started in iMovie 2024:

1. Launch iMovie on the device you are using.
2. Navigate to the "**File**" menu and check the box next to "**New Project**."
3. Pick the project template that is most suitable for your requirements, or pick "**Blank Project**" to begin the customizing process in its entirety.
4. Give your project a name and choose a place to store it.

Adding Collaborators

When you have finished developing your idea, it is time to seek out potential partners. In this manner:

1. Navigate to the user interface of iMovie and click on the "**Collaborate**" button that is situated in the upper-right-hand corner.

2. Either choose the email addresses of your colleagues from your contacts or enter their electronic mail addresses.
3. Personalize the access permissions for each collaborator, specifying whether they can modify or merely see the content.
4. To invite members of the team to participate in the project, click the "**Send Invitation**" button.

Collaborating in Real-Time

Following the acceptance of the invitation by your colleagues, you will be able to begin working together in real-time shortly.

In iMovie 2024, the following are among the most important capabilities for collaborative editing:

1. **Real-Time Sync**: Any changes made by one collaborator are immediately reflected by the other collaborators, guaranteeing that synchronization is carried out without any interruptions.
2. **Comments and Annotations**: Collaborators can post comments and annotations on certain clips or segments, which makes communication and feedback easier to do.
3. **Version History**: iMovie has a feature that preserves version history automatically, which enables you to restore to earlier versions of your video if necessary.
4. **Chat capability**: The built-in chat capability provides real-time communication between collaborators, which improves the ability to work together and improves cooperation.

Sharing and Exporting Projects

When the project that you and your team have been working on together is finished, it is time to make it public. In this manner:

1. Place your cursor over the "**Share**" button that is situated in the upper-right-hand corner of the iMovie interface.
2. Make your selection for the export format that you want to use, such as a file, YouTube, Vimeo, or iCloud.
3. Make individual adjustments to the export parameters, including the resolution, frame rate, and compression options.
4. To produce the final result, click the "**Export**" button.

Best Practices for Collaborative Editing

It is important to take into consideration the following best practices to promote seamless communication and maximum productivity:

1. One of the most important things to remember is to have an open line of communication with your partners for the whole of the project.

2. The second step is to establish workflow guidelines, which include defining roles, responsibilities, and procedures to simplify the editing process.
3. To ensure that everyone stays on track, it is important to establish clear deadlines for the various project milestones.
4. It is important to encourage input from collaborators and to be open to making modifications based on constructive criticism offered by others.
5. Always be sure to back up your project files to avoid losing any data and to guarantee continuity.

CHAPTER THIRTEEN
CUSTOM EXPORT FORMATS

Overview

Chapter thirteen talks about custom export formats including working with aspect ratio, changing aspect ratio with keynote, using handbrake, and so much more.

How to work with aspect ratio

You have the option to choose from a variety of aspect ratios that are suggested by previous versions of the iMovie program for Mac devices. On the other hand, you are only able to choose between the normal 4:3 aspect ratio and the widescreen 16:9 aspect ratio. The process involves uploading the movie, selecting ProjectProperties from the menu that appears, and then selecting the desired option.

On the other hand, to use iMovie 10 or later, you will need to follow these steps:

1. The first step is to launch the iMovie application and then choose the **"Create New" button** located in the upper-left corner of your screen.

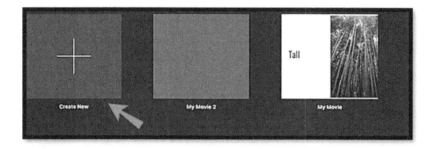

2. Choose **"Movie"** from the menu that drops down.

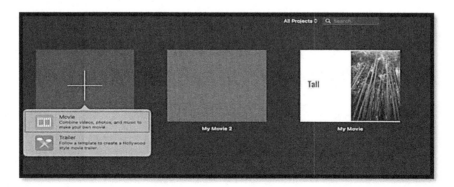

3. You can upload a video from your device by clicking the **"Import Media"** button. In addition, you can easily transfer video clips from the web to the timeline of iMovie by dragging and dropping them.

4. At the top of the toolbar, choose the **"Crop"** icon and click on it.

5. Move the boundaries of the window that has been cropped across your video screen.

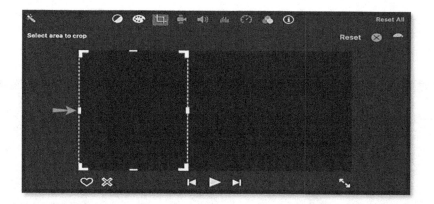

6. After you have finished, you should click on the blue checkmark button that is located in the top-right corner of your video.
7. Click the "**Share**" button located in the top-right corner of the screen.

8. Proceed to save the video.

How to change aspect ratio with keynote

Having a solid understanding of what aspect ratio comprises is very necessary before delving into the technical aspects. There is a proportionate connection between the width and height of an image or video, and this relationship is referred to as the aspect ratio. Aspect ratios such as 16:9 (widescreen), 4:3 (standard), and a variety of cinematic ratios such as 2.35:1 are examples of common aspect ratios. Considering that various platforms and media often have certain aspect ratio requirements, the ability to change properly is very necessary to preserve the visual integrity of the content.

What Functions Do Keynote and iMovie Serve

It's possible that the presentation software that Apple offers, Keynote, may not seem to be the most apparent option for video editing. On the other hand, its extensive capabilities go beyond slideshows and provide opportunities for creative expression in the context of multimedia projects. On the other hand, iMovie is a video editing tool that is designed to be user-friendly and is well-known for its simplicity and efficiency. The combination of the two allows users to generate dynamic outcomes, including the ability to easily modify aspect ratios if they so want.

The steps

1. Start Keynote on your Mac and open it.
2. To create a new presentation, pick "**New**" from the "**File**" menu.
3. Depending on your style, you can either begin with a blank slide or choose a theme to use.
4. Go to the "**Document**" tab located on the top menu bar.
5. Choose "**Slide Size**" from the dropdown menu, and then choose "**Custom Slide Size**" from the menu that appears.
6. The measurements that correspond to the aspect ratio that you want to use should be entered. To give you an example, you may input 1920 pixels by 1080 pixels if you want to choose a 16:9 aspect ratio.
7. Personalize your presentations by adding photos, text, graphics, or any other components that are pertinent to the project you are working on.
8. As you create, be sure to keep the new aspect ratio in mind and make sure that your content can properly fit inside the frame.
9. When you have reached a point where you are content with the slides using Keynote, it is time to export them as a video. Navigate to the "**File**" menu and then pick "**Export To**" follow by "**Movie**." Make the selections for the video quality and resolution that you want to use.
10. To save your Keynote presentation as a video file on your computer, press the "**Next**" button and then the "**Export**" button.
11. If you wish to modify the aspect ratio of an existing project, you can either start a new project or open an existing one.

12. To import your Keynote video, select "**Movie**" from the drop-down menu that appears after clicking on the "+" symbol located in the top left corner of the iMovie interface.
13. If the aspect ratio does not match the parameters for your project, the movie will most likely appear with black bars or letterboxing after it has been imported into iMovie.
14. Clicking on the video clip in the timeline will allow you to make adjustments to the aspect ratio. Choose the "**Crop to Fill**" option from the dropdown menu that is located in the preview window. Since this is the case, you will be able to zoom in on the video and modify the frame so that it conforms to the aspect ratio that you choose.
15. To check that the aspect ratio modification seems to be adequate, you should play through the video that you have altered. It is necessary to make any extra modifications or upgrades that may be required, such as the inclusion of transitions, effects, or audio.
16. Export your completed film from iMovie after you have reached a point where you are satisfied with the outcome.
17. Using the "**File**" menu, pick "**Share**" and then "**File**." This will provide the desired result. Make your selections for the export parameters you want, including the resolution and the file format.
18. To store your movie on your computer, you will need to give it a name and choose a location to save it. To export your movie from iMovie, click "**Next**" and then "**Save**" after that.

Installing and running handbrake

The process of uploading and downloading large video files is a pain. The popular program known as Handbrake can dramatically reduce the size of files without compromising their quality. What makes it such a popular choice? Video files can be converted from almost any format, it is completely free and open-source, and it is compatible with Windows, Mac OS X, and Linux.

What exactly is the hand brake?

HandBrake is a well-liked video editing program that is used by both novices and professionals alike. Windows, Mac OS X, and Linux users may all use it, and it is completely free and open-source. The primary function is to reduce the size of video files without compromising their quality. You can also extract audio, convert formats, optimize for a variety of devices, trim and resize frames, and optimize for various devices.

This software offers a user interface that is easy to understand, which makes it very easy to navigate. In addition to that, it is equipped with sophisticated capabilities such as support for multiple audio tracks, customized video filters, and subtitles. Gain access to a free download and immediately begin improving your video experience.

Why Should People Compress Videos Use HandBrake Videos?

Using HandBrake to compress movies is a strategic choice that is motivated by multiple compelling factors, including the following:

- **Optimizing Storage Space:** Video files have the potential to use up a large amount of storage space. You can maximize the amount of storage space available by compressing them with HandBrake. As a result, precious storage space is made available for more material.
- **Bandwidth Efficiency**: Compressed movies use less bandwidth, which lessens the burden that is placed on networks when streaming. This is one of the benefits of bandwidth efficiency. The techniques that HandBrake uses to compress files guarantee that playing experiences are smoother. It is particularly important to keep this in mind in situations when internet availability is restricted.
- **Quality Preservation**: HandBrake is exceptional in its ability to maintain video quality while simultaneously optimizing file sizes. Users can get the advantages of compression without sacrificing the quality of the visual material shown.

Steps to Use HandBrake to Compress Video

Handbrake is a free program that can be used on both Macs and PCs. It reduces the size of files while preserving the quality of the images and sounds.

Where can I find it? To proceed, just follow the instructions below:

1. First, go to the official website and download the Handbrake application.

2. Launch the Handbrake program on the device you now own.
3. Navigate to the File menu. Click the **Open Source button** next.
4. Choosing your video file.
5. To go to the fifth step, open the Presets menu and choose Fast 1080p30.
6. Navigate to the Video tab and check that the following settings are correct:
- H.264 is the video encoder
- Constant Quality, RF 22
- FPS: Same as source. Constant Framerate

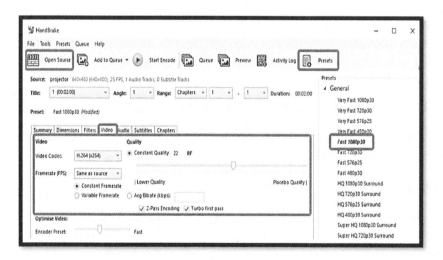

You have the option of lowering the frame rate to 15 or lower if your movie has very little motion. This is an optional approach.

7. Select **Browse** to select a place to store the file and a name for the file.
8. Go to the Audio tab and make sure that the Bitrate option is set to 192 (or 160).

9. Use the "**Add to Queue**" button. To enter more films, you may repeat steps 3-9 as many times as necessary.
10. To start the encoding process, go to Step 10 and click the **green Start Encode button**.
11. Your movies will be compressed into the MP4 format after some time has passed. These shorter films may then be uploaded to the area where you save your files.

Issues and Ways While Processing HandBrake File Compression

Do you have difficulties while attempting to compress files with HandBrake? Try not to worry; you are not the only one. It may be quite aggravating when problems arise during the compression process. The key to attaining outcomes that are smooth and efficient is to first identify the issues and then find solutions to them.

To begin, the following is a list of the most typical problems that occur when HandBrake is used to compress videos:

- **Quality Loss**: The compression process might sometimes result in a deterioration of quality.
- **Incomplete Compression**: On the other hand, incomplete compression refers to files that are not completely compressed or that do not finish the process.
- **Audio Sync Issues:** The compressed video may have issues with the audio synchronization, which are referred to as "**audio sync issues**."
- **Unsupported Formats:** Difficulties in managing certain input or output formats are referred to as "**unsupported file formats**."

How to add a source to the handbrake

Before you can add a source to Handbrake in iMovie 2024, you will first need to make sure that your computer is equipped with the appropriate software and files. The video transcoder known as Handbrake is quite popular, and the video editing software known as iMovie is frequently used on devices running macOS and iOS. When you combine the power of iMovie's editing features with the encoding capabilities of Handbrake, you can greatly improve the quality of your video production process.

1. If you have not yet installed Handbrake on your computer, you should go to the official website for Handbrake, which is located at handbrake.fr, and download the version that is compatible with your operating system. Therefore, you must download the appropriate version of Handbrake, which is available for macOS, Windows, and Linux.

When the download is finished, you should proceed with the installation by following the instructions that the installer gives you. Once the installation is complete, you are prepared to proceed to the subsequent step.

2. To make use of Handbrake with iMovie, you will first require a video file that you can work with. iMovie should be launched on your macOS device and the project that you wish to export should be opened. First, select the clip or clips that you wish to export, then go to the "**File**" menu and select "**Share**" > "**File**" from the dropdown menu that appears. You will be presented with a dialogue box that allows you to customize the export settings when you take this action.

3. You can make adjustments to a variety of parameters, including resolution, quality, and file format, within the export settings dialogue box. You must select a format that is compatible with Handbrake, such as MP4, MKV, or MOV among others. It is recommended that you click the "**Next**" button once you have finished configuring the settings to your liking. Select a folder that will serve as the destination for the exported video, and then click the "**Save**" button to begin the process of exporting the video. The length of time required for this process is contingent on the complexity and length of the video you are working on.

4. Once the export procedure has been finished, you will need to locate the video file that was exported on your computer. At this point, it is time to engage the handbrake.

Handbrake can be launched by selecting the shortcut on your desktop or the applications folder on your computer. Handbrake's intuitive user interface will be presented to you as soon as it is installed and operational. To open the source code of the video that you exported from iMovie, click the "**Open Source**" button in the Handbrake interface and then navigate to the location where you saved the video. To load the file into Handbrake, select the file and then click the "**Open**" button.

5. After you have loaded your source video into Handbrake, you will now have the ability to customize the encoding settings to satisfy your individual preferences. When it comes to modifying video quality, resolution, codec, and other aspects, Handbrake provides a wide variety of modification options.

Experiment with a variety of settings to find the optimal balance between the size of the file and the quality of the video. Bear in mind that higher quality settings will result in larger file sizes, whereas lower quality settings will reduce file size but may sacrifice video clarity. Therefore, it is important to keep this in mind.

6. Once you have determined that the encoding settings are satisfactory, select a destination folder for the encoded file by clicking on the "**Browse**" button located within the interface of the Handbrake application. Make a selection on your computer to determine the location where you would like to save the encoded video.

Finally, to initiate the transcoding process, you will need to click on the **"Start Encode"** button within Handbrake. This process may take some time to finish taking into consideration the length and complexity of your video.

7. After Handbrake has completed the process of encoding the video, you will need to navigate to the destination folder where you have saved the encoded file. You can now import this file into iMovie so that you can continue editing it or share it with others.

iMovie should be launched, and the project that you want to add the encoded video should be opened. When you want to import media into iMovie, you must first click the "+" button in the timeline, and then navigate to the location on your computer where the encoded video file is stored. To incorporate the file into your iMovie project, select it and then click the **"Import"** button. It is now possible to use the editing tools that are included in iMovie to further improve your video by adding effects, transitions, and audio.

CHAPTER FOURTEEN
INTEGRATING KEYNOTE

Overview

In this chapter, you will learn how to integrate keynote into iMovie, how to export keynote titles, how to export transparency and so many other functions.

How to create custom titles with keynote

Crafting personalized titles using Keynote and seamlessly incorporating them into iMovie can elevate the quality of your videos, enhancing their ability to effectively convey information and establish the desired atmosphere. Now, we can explore the detailed process of achieving this in iMovie 2024.

Creating the Title Slide in Keynote

1. **Start Keynote**: Access Keynote on your Mac. If you don't have it installed, you can easily download it from the Mac App Store.
2. **Choose a Theme:** Pick a theme that perfectly matches the style of your video. Keynote provides a wide selection of pre-designed themes for users to choose from. If you prefer, you can also begin with a blank slide and design it from scratch.
3. **Customize Your Title Slide:** Simply click on the text boxes on the slide to make changes. Feel free to personalize the text by adjusting the font, size, color, and alignment to suit your preferences. It would be beneficial to include your brand colors or any design elements that are relevant to your video.
4. **Add Effects or Graphics**: Enhance your title slide by incorporating graphics, shapes, or animations to make it more visually appealing. The Keynote software offers a variety of choices to enhance the visual appeal of your title.
5. **Save your Slide**: Make sure to save your slide as an image file once you're happy with the design. To export your file as an image, navigate to the File menu and select **Export To**, then choose the desired format such as JPEG or PNG. Make sure to save the image in a convenient location for future access.

Importing the Title Slide into iMovie

1. Startup iMovie on your Mac.
2. Select "**Create New**" to initiate a new project or access an existing project in which you wish to include a personalized title.
3. Find the image of the title slide that you saved from Keynote. Simply drag and drop it into the iMovie project timeline at the desired location for the title to appear. In another approach, you have the option to navigate to File > Import Media and choose the title slide image from your computer.

Adding Text Overlay in iMovie

1. To select the Title Slide, simply click on the image of the title slide in the timeline.
2. To access the Text Tools, simply click on the "T" icon in the toolbar above the viewer.
3. To add text overlay, simply click on the title slide in the viewer at the desired location. A text box will be displayed. Please enter the text you would like to use for the title, subtitle, or any other additional information.
4. To give your text a personal touch, simply select the desired text and use the formatting options available in the text tools toolbar. You can modify the font, size, color, and alignment, and apply effects such as bold or italic.
5. Simply drag the text box to place it on the title slide. To resize the text box, simply click and drag the handles located around the edges.
6. If necessary, you can adjust the timing of the title slide by simply clicking and dragging its edges in the timeline. This will allow you to make it longer or shorter as needed.

Review and Complete

1. Try playing through your project to get a preview of how the custom title slide will appear in your video.
2. Make necessary adjustments: If needed, make any changes to the text, formatting, or timing until you are happy with the outcome.
3. After you have carefully crafted your custom title slide and positioned it just right in your video, it's time to save your project and exports it in the format of your choice. To export the video file to your computer, navigate to **File**, then select **Share**, and finally choose **File**.

How to export keynote titles

Understanding the basics of Keynote titles in iMovie is crucial before proceeding with the export process. Keynote, Apple's presentation software, enables users to create visually captivating slides with customizable text, graphics, and animations. iMovie allows users to easily import Keynote presentations and use them as dynamic titles and overlays in their videos. This integration allows creators to enhance their projects with a polished look, enhancing the overall visual appeal and engagement.

Here are the steps:

1. To export Keynote titles in iMovie, start by crafting engaging titles directly in Keynote. Open **Keynote** and start by choosing a theme that suits your presentation. Ensure that the slide layout, text styles, and graphical elements are perfectly in sync with the aesthetic of your video project. Add animations and transitions to enhance the visual appeal and style of your titles. After you have finished creating your Keynote presentation, make sure to save it in a compatible format like .key or .pdf. Make sure to arrange your slides in a clear and organized manner, so that each title or graphic can be easily recognized and used in iMovie.

2. Now that your Keynote presentation is all set, it's time to bring it into iMovie. Open iMovie and access your project or start a new one. Go to the location where you saved your Keynote presentation and choose the file you want to import. When using iMovie, you will be prompted to select your preferred method of importing the Keynote presentation. Choose the option that aligns with your requirements, such as importing each slide as separate clips or importing only specific slides. Take into account the pacing and flow of your video project when making this decision.

3. After importing your Keynote presentation into iMovie, you can start integrating the titles into your project. Arrange the Keynote clips by dragging and dropping them onto the timeline, making sure they match up with the relevant parts of your video. Make sure to adjust the duration of each Keynote title clip so that it blends smoothly with the pacing of your video. Feel free to adjust the clips to fit your desired timing and create the desired impact. Trimming, splitting, or extending the duration are all options at your disposal.

4. Once you've added the Keynote titles to your iMovie project, you have the flexibility to personalize them and make them more visually appealing, ensuring they blend seamlessly with your video content. To access the editing options available in iMovie, simply select each Keynote title clip on the timeline. Play around with different text styles, fonts, colors, and sizes to make sure the titles are easy to read and visually captivating. Elevate the quality of your Keynote titles by applying transitions and effects that enhance their visual appeal and align them seamlessly with the overall aesthetic of your video.

5. After you've put the finishing touches on your iMovie project by adding Keynote titles, it's time to export it as a final video format. To share your project in iMovie, simply navigate to the "**File**" menu and choose the "**Share**" option. Select the preferred export settings, such as the video resolution, quality, and file format. Make sure to select the "**Include Keynote Titles**" option before proceeding with the export process. The inclusion of Keynote titles in the final exported video by iMovie guarantees that the visual enhancements you've made to your project are preserved.

How to create animated titles in a keynote

Create the first scene

To begin crafting your new title, start by selecting a theme in Keynote and designing a background. First, open Keynote on your Mac. Keynote presents you with the typical macOS dialog for choosing a file. Find the **New Document button** and click on it.

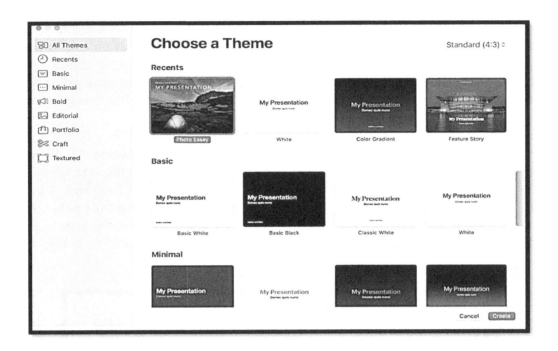

Keynote requires you to select a theme to use. If you're looking to create animated titles with photos as a background, the Photo Essay theme is a great place to start. It is important to consider the aspect ratio you want to use for your titles. To select the standard 4:3 format for your video, simply click on the option located in the upper-right corner. For those dealing with HD (1080p or 720p) or 4K video, the recommended option is Wide (16:9). After selecting the theme and aspect ratio, simply click on the **Create button**. An empty slide is displayed.

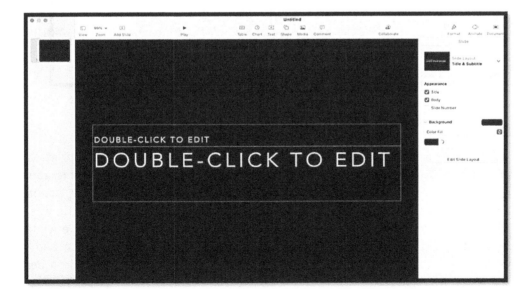

This is an excellent choice for our first slide. We would like to begin with a black background. Click on each of the text box placeholders displayed above. Press the Delete key on your keyboard when the handles, which are small square boxes on the perimeter of the text box, appear. Ensure that both text boxes are modified accordingly to achieve a black background. Now, let's proceed to include a new slide. To add a slide, simply click on the "**Add Slide**" button located in the toolbar above the slide. A variety of slide types are available.

- **Proceed to choose a photo**

The Photo slide contains a placeholder image that does not meet our requirements. We would like to import an image from our library. To access the background photo on the slide, simply click on it. Next, navigate to the Image tab located in the sidebar on the right-hand side. A button labeled "**Replace**" appears. Click it and select your photo using the standard file picker. Make adjustments to the exposure and saturation as necessary. After selecting the image for the Keynote presentation, we adjusted the Exposure slider to enhance the brightness of the image. Here is a description of the second scene as it stands:

- **Add text boxes**

Currently, we are considering incorporating some text boxes to display my initial titles. Start by clicking the **Text button** located in the top toolbar. This action will cause a text box to appear on the screen. Choose a font family, typeface, color, and size from the Text tab in the sidebar. The top line of text was chosen to be Avenir Black 36 points in red, while the main title was set to Avenir Black 60 points in black. We enhanced the visibility of the text by applying a white Drop Shadow to each text box after selecting them since the title image is black and white. Experimenting with the blur, offset, angle, and opacity of the shadow resulted in a desirable effect:

- **Add another photo slide**

Now, include another photo slide using the same process mentioned before. For this particular situation, we would like to include a compilation of national parks on the slide. To create a non-bulleted list, simply press **Return** after each park name. Adding a black shadow to the text enhances its readability against the picture background.

Adding animation: transitions

Choose dissolve as the transition for the first two slides. Currently, the slideshow is quite dull, but we can make it more engaging by incorporating animated transitions and builds. The difference lies in the occurrence between two slides and within a single slide. For instance, one could smoothly transition from one slide to the next and incorporate text with unique animations that appear at different times. The first slide was made black to create a sense of drama. We prefer for it to remain on the screen momentarily before gradually transitioning into the initial titles. To accomplish this, select the initial slide and proceed to click on the Animate button located on the toolbar. Now, go ahead and click on the **Add an Effect button**. Keynote offers a variety of transition effects to choose from. We selected **Dissolve**. When you're experimenting, it can be helpful to try out various transitions by selecting them and previewing the effect. Experimenting with the Duration and Delay can be quite beneficial. The Duration refers to the length of time it takes for the transition to be completed, while Delay indicates the period that the transition "**holds**" before it begins. Additionally, remember to choose the "**Automatically**" option for the Start Transition.

Adding animation: builds

To begin the build, simply click on the subtitle and then choose an effect from the Build In tab. The Trace effect is quite impressive, resembling the meticulous art of lettering done with drafting tools on the screen. Just like before, it's crucial to carefully choose the direction and duration for the effect. We chose a Dissolve effect from the Build Out tab. The titles are displayed on the screen, linger for a brief moment, and then fade away. It is advisable to always use the "**Automatically**" option under "**Start Transition**" in all scenarios. Lastly, and to maintain a smooth flow, we refrained from demonstrating the addition of a sophisticated Lens Flare Build In effect on the final slide.

Create a movie

By now, we are confident that you understand how to add and preview different effects for builds and transitions. Once you believe your titles are finished, simply click the Play button located on the toolbar to preview them. Please be aware that you will need to click to progress through the builds, although the transitions will happen automatically. Once we are satisfied with the final product, we can proceed to export our titles as a movie. To export your Keynote presentation as a movie, go to the **Keynote menu** and select **File**, then **Export to**, and finally **Movie**.

Movie export settings

Exporting as a movie automatically defaults to the Self-Playing option. Make sure to select all slides, specify a timing for the Keynote to transition to the next slide or build, and choose a resolution. The resolution of 1024×768 was chosen, but feel free to adjust it to match the video you are adding titles. Proceed to the next step, select a suitable location and name for the file, and then start the process.

How to use magic move animations

Let's start by understanding the concept behind Magic Move animations before delving into their intricacies. The Magic Move transition effect in iMovie allows for the creation of smooth and seamless transitions between two clips or images. The process involves analyzing the content of the initial clip or image and then skillfully animating the transition to the subsequent clip or image, resulting in a visually captivating effect.

Here are the steps to get started with Magic Move animations in iMovie 2024:

1. To open iMovie, simply launch the iMovie application on your Mac or iOS device.
2. Whether you're starting from scratch or working with an existing project, you can seamlessly integrate Magic Move animations.

3. Add the video clips or images you wish to include in your project to the iMovie timeline.
4. Organize the clips or images in the preferred sequence on the timeline, ensuring seamless flow between scenes.

Using Magic Move Animations

Now that your media is organized, it's time to add some Magic Move animations:

1. To select the first clip or image, simply click on it in the timeline.
2. To access the Transitions Menu, simply click on the **"Transitions"** button located in the toolbar above the preview window.
3. Select "**Magic Move**" from the list of transition options.
4. To adjust the duration of the Magic Move transition, simply click on the transition icon in the timeline and drag its edges to make it shorter or longer.
5. To make precise adjustments, select the transition icon in the timeline and access the Inspector window. From there, you can fine-tune settings like start and end positions, opacity, and more.
6. For subsequent clips or images, simply follow the same steps mentioned above to transition between each pair.

Tips for Creating Powerful Magic Move Animations

For optimal use of Magic Move animations, take into account the following suggestions:

1. Maintain a consistent style and theme throughout your project to ensure that Magic Move transitions flow seamlessly.
2. To achieve the best outcomes, it is recommended to utilize video clips and images with high resolution that are visually captivating and clear.
3. Consider trying out various transition durations to discover the timing that enhances your content the most.
4. Move animations with the addition of text overlays, filters, and various effects, resulting in more captivating videos.
5. It's always a good idea to review your project and see how the Magic Move animations come together. Make any necessary adjustments to ensure a polished final product.

Advanced Techniques

If you're eager to elevate your Magic Move animations, here are some advanced techniques to explore:

1. **Layering Effects**: Experiment with layering multiple clips or images to create intricate animations with depth and dimension.
2. **Masking and Green Screen:** Using the power of masking and green screen techniques to effortlessly blend Magic Move animations, resulting in captivating visual effects and smooth transitions.

3. **Sound Design**: Take your Magic Move animations to the next level by incorporating personalized sound effects and music, creating a truly immersive experience for your audience.
4. **Motion Tracking:** Discover the power of motion tracking to bring life to your clips or images, injecting a sense of dynamic movement into your Magic Move transitions.

How to export transparency in video

The concept of transparency in video involves the visual effect of being able to see through specific sections of a video layer, which enables the display of underlying layers or backgrounds.

This feature is frequently used for overlays, logos, titles, and animations, allowing the content to seamlessly merge with the background.

1. First, you'll want to start by creating your project in iMovie. Before delving into exporting with transparency, it is essential to first create your project in iMovie. To get started, open iMovie on your Mac. From there, you can either begin a new project or access an existing one that already contains the elements you want to export with transparency.
2. To export transparency in a video, it is necessary to have elements with transparent backgrounds already included in your project. These elements can be PNG images or videos with alpha channels. To incorporate these transparent assets into your iMovie project, simply click on the "**Import Media**" button and choose the desired files from your computer.
3. Organize the transparent elements on the timeline according to the desired sequence for your final video. The layer-based approach in iMovie ensures that elements placed higher on the timeline will appear on top of those below them.
4. To adjust the transparency of an element in your video, simply select the element on the timeline and click on the "Adjust" button. You have the option to modify the opacity slider to increase or decrease the transparency of the element.

After you've carefully organized your elements, it's time to export your video with transparency.

Here's a step-by-step guide on how to do it in iMovie 2024:

- To access the menu options, locate the "**File**" button positioned in the top-left corner of the screen.
- Choose "**Share**" from the dropdown menu.
- Select "**File**" from the sharing options.
- Ensure that the "**Video Quality**" in the export settings window is set to "**Best (ProRes 4444)**".
- Select the option "**Export with Transparency**" by checking the corresponding box.

153

5. Once you've chosen to export with transparency, you'll be able to select the destination for saving your video file. In addition, you have the flexibility to customize various export settings to suit your preferences, including resolution, frame rate, and codec options.

6. After configuring the export settings to your preference, simply click on the "**Next**" button to initiate the video export process with transparency. The processing of your project in iMovie will result in the creation of a video file that includes transparency.

7. Once the export process is finished, you can confirm the preservation of transparency in your video by opening it in a video player or editing software that supports this feature. The transparent elements should appear as intended, allowing the background to show through.

Exporting and importing multi-stage magic move animations

Before we dive into the world of exporting and importing multi-stage Magic Move animations, it's crucial to understand their core concept. The beauty of multi-stage Magic Move animations lies in their ability to seamlessly integrate multiple elements within a single transition, setting them apart from traditional animations that involve simple transitions between clips. The seamless transitions between clips and the ability for individual elements to animate within those clips create a captivating visual experience.

Developing Multi-Stage Magic Move Animations

To fully use the potential of multi-stage Magic Move animations, it is essential to create your masterpiece within iMovie. Start by importing your media assets, such as videos, images, and audio, into your project timeline. After that, organize these elements in a way that effectively conveys your story, making sure to create seamless transitions between scenes. Now that you have set up your basic timeline, it's time to explore the captivating world of multi-stage animations. To animate the clip or image of your choice, go to the "**Animations**" tab. Here, you'll discover a wide range of animation options, including Magic Move. Opt for this option and customize your animation settings to align with your creative vision. Now, let's explore the exciting aspect of incorporating multiple stages into your animation. The interface of iMovie 2024 is designed to be user-friendly, allowing you to easily add keyframes to your animation timeline and specify the exact points for element animation. The range of possibilities is truly limitless, whether it's a gradual zoom, a subtle rotation, or a dramatic pan. Through careful placement of keyframes and precise adjustments to their parameters, you have the power to create captivating multi-stage animations that will truly captivate your audience's imagination. Explore various timing, easing, and motion options to achieve the desired effect, honing your animation until it seamlessly aligns with your narrative vision.

Exporting Multi-Stage Magic Move Animations

After finishing your multi-stage Magic Move animation, it's time to showcase your creation to the world. The process of exporting animations in iMovie 2024 is designed to be user-friendly and efficient, making it easy to incorporate into your workflow. To get started, choose the section of your project that includes the multi-stage animation you want to export. The inclusion of only the desired segment in the final export helps to minimize file size and optimize playback performance. Once you have selected your animation segment, simply go to the **"File"** menu and click on **"Export"**. Discover a wide range of export presets designed specifically for various platforms and resolutions. Choose the preset that aligns with your requirements or personalize the export settings to precisely adjust the output according to your preferences. Take a moment to review your settings and ensure everything is configured to your satisfaction before finalizing the export process. Make sure to carefully review the export resolution, file format, and compression settings to prevent any unexpected issues in the future. After you've made sure your settings are just right, simply click the **"Export"** button and witness the impressive capabilities of iMovie as it transforms your intricate animation into a high-quality video file, ready to be shared with others. This process may take some time, depending on the complexity of your animation and the power of your hardware. So, take a moment to sit back, relax, and enjoy the anticipation of unveiling your creation to the world.

Importing Multi-Stage Magic Move Animations

After successfully exporting your multi-stage Magic Move animation, it's time to incorporate it into your wider creative projects. iMovie 2024 simplifies the importing process, whether you're combining multiple animations into a single project or incorporating them into a larger multimedia production. To begin, open the project where you want to import your animation. Whether you're starting a new project or working on an existing one, it all depends on your workflow and creative objectives. After that, find the directory where your exported animation file is saved and proceed to import it into your iMovie project. Drag and drop the file into the project timeline to seamlessly align it with the rest of your content. After importing, the multi-stage Magic Move animation will seamlessly fit into your project timeline, ready to seamlessly blend into your narrative. The placement, duration, and timing of the element can be customized to seamlessly integrate with the surrounding elements, resulting in a cohesive storytelling experience from start to finish. After successfully importing your animation, take a moment to preview your project and appreciate the results of your hard work. Appreciate the smooth transitions, the effortless motion, and the captivating storytelling enabled by iMovie 2024's multi-stage Magic Move animations.

CHAPTER FIFTEEN
TIPS AND TROUBLESHOOTING

Overview

We have come to the end of this guide. The last chapter widely focuses on the tips and tricks that can make you better with iMovie as well as the various troubleshooting issues and their solutions.

FAQ and answers regarding iMovie

Every iMovie user has come across these questions and we are here to provide solutions:

- **What exactly is iMovie?**

iMovie is a video editing software created by Apple Inc. It is compatible with macOS, iOS, and iPadOS devices. iMovie provides users with a seamless experience for video editing, incorporating special effects, crafting trailers, and effortlessly sharing their creative projects.

- **Is iMovie available for free?**

Indeed, iMovie can be downloaded and used for free by Apple device owners. It is included as a standard feature on the majority of Mac computers and iOS devices, including iPhones and iPads. If you don't have it pre-installed, you have the option to download it for free from the Mac App Store or the App Store on iOS devices.

- **Can I use iMovie on Windows?**

Regrettably, iMovie is exclusively compatible with macOS, iOS, and iPadOS devices. Unfortunately, Windows users do not have access to an official version of iMovie. Nonetheless, Windows users have the option to explore alternative video editing software that provides comparable features to iMovie.

- **What are the system requirements for iMovie?**

The system requirements for iMovie can vary depending on the device you're using:

1. Mac users will need to have macOS 10.15.6 or a newer version installed, along with a minimum of 2GB of RAM (4GB is recommended) to use iMovie.
2. iMovie is compatible with iPhone, iPad, and iPod touch, and requires iOS 13.4 or later.
3. iPadOS: iMovie is compatible with iPadOS 13.4 or newer versions.

- **What are the features and capabilities of iMovie?**

iMovie provides a wide array of features that enable you to produce videos with a polished and professional appearance.

- **Video Editing**: Easily trim, split, and arrange clips on a timeline.
- **Add Effects:** Enhance your videos with filters, transitions, titles, and music to add a touch of creativity.
- **Create Trailers:** Select from a range of templates to produce captivating Hollywood-style trailers.
- **Share**: Easily share your videos on social media platforms or export them in a variety of formats.

- **Can videos from other sources be imported into iMovie?**

iMovie offers the convenience of importing videos from various sources, such as your device's camera roll, external hard drives, or other storage devices. In addition, videos can be imported from iCloud Drive or directly from compatible cameras.

- **Does iMovie support 4K video editing?**

Indeed, iMovie is capable of editing videos in 4K resolution. Experience high-quality viewing by editing, exporting, and sharing videos in 4K resolution.

- **Can I use iMovie for professional video editing?**

Although iMovie is a powerful video editing tool, its main focus is on catering to casual users and enthusiasts. Experienced video editors may find its features somewhat limited in comparison to more advanced editing software such as Final Cut Pro X. Although iMovie is a fantastic choice for newcomers, it can deliver exceptional outcomes.

- **Is iMovie user-friendly for beginners?**

The user-friendly interface of iMovie makes it easy for beginners to learn the basics of video editing. The software provides user-friendly tools and features, including drag-and-drop functionality and built-in tutorials, to assist users in getting started easily.

- **Can I add music to my videos using iMovie?**

iMovie offers the option to enhance your videos with music either from your iTunes library or by selecting from a variety of preloaded soundtracks and sound effects. Additionally, you have the option to record your voiceover directly within the app.

- **Does iMovie provide technical support?**

Apple offers technical support for iMovie through a range of channels, such as online resources, community forums, and customer support. Help documentation and tutorials are conveniently accessible within the iMovie app.

- **Can I use iMovie to edit videos for YouTube?**

iMovie is widely used for editing videos for YouTube. The app allows you to easily edit your videos, including adding titles and effects and exporting them in formats that are perfect for uploading directly to YouTube.

- **Is iMovie a safe option for downloading and using?**

Indeed, iMovie is developed by Apple Inc., a highly regarded company renowned for its dedication to security and privacy. The software is consistently updated to ensure it remains secure and can be safely downloaded and used on your Apple devices.

- **Can I use iMovie for editing videos intended for commercial use?**

Indeed, iMovie is a versatile tool that allows you to edit videos for various commercial purposes. You can use it to create compelling promotional videos for your business or to skillfully edit footage for client projects. It is important to keep in mind Apple's terms of service and any licensing restrictions that may apply to the content you use in your videos.

- **How frequently does iMovie receive updates?**

iMovie is updated in sync with major macOS and iOS releases, which happen yearly. The updates may include new features, performance improvements, and bug fixes to enhance the user experience.

- **Is it possible to use iMovie without an Apple ID?**

Although it is feasible to use iMovie without an Apple ID, having one is necessary for downloading the app from the App Store accessing specific features like iCloud integration, and sharing videos to social media platforms. It's free to create an Apple ID and the process only requires a few minutes of your time.

- **Is iMovie offered in different languages?**

iMovie is available in a wide range of languages, such as English, Spanish, French, German, Japanese, Chinese, and more. The app allows you to customize the language settings according to your preferences.

- **Does iMovie have support for third-party plugins?**

Unfortunately, iMovie cannot support third-party plugins or extensions. The software offers a range of pre-installed features and effects for editing your videos.

- **Can I edit videos offline using iMovie?**

Indeed, iMovie is specifically designed to function without an internet connection, enabling you to effortlessly edit videos offline. Some features, like iCloud integration and sharing to social media platforms, may need an internet connection.

- **Where can I find tutorials and resources to learn iMovie?**

Numerous tutorials and resources can be found online to assist you in learning iMovie. These include video tutorials on YouTube, Apple's official iMovie support page, and community forums where you can seek advice and ask questions from fellow users.

Addressing common iMovie issues and providing solutions

Importing Media Files

Issue: Having difficulty importing media files into iMovie.
Here's a solution:

- Make sure the media files are compatible with iMovie. iMovie is compatible with a wide range of file formats, including MP4, MOV, M4V, and more. Make sure your media files are in one of these formats.
- Make sure to update iMovie to the latest version. Occasionally, older software versions can encounter compatibility problems.
- Try restarting your computer and attempting to import the media files once more.
- If the issue continues, you may want to think about using third-party software to convert the media files to a compatible format before importing them into iMovie.
3. **Issue**: iMovie unexpectedly crashes or freezes while editing.

Here's a solution:

- Make sure to close any other applications running in the background to free up system resources.
- Make sure to regularly check for updates and install the latest version of iMovie. Updates often come with bug fixes that improve stability.
- Make sure to restart your computer to refresh system processes and clear temporary files.
- If you're still experiencing issues, you may want to try reinstalling iMovie. This can help fix any potential problems with corrupted files or configurations.

4. **Problems with Audio Synchronization**

Issue: Audio and video synchronization is lost after editing.

Here's a solution:
- Make sure to check the alignment of the audio and video clips in the timeline.
- Make sure to trim or adjust the clips to properly synchronize the audio with the corresponding video.
- Make sure to disable any audio effects or enhancements applied to the clips to avoid synchronization issues.
- If the problem continues, you can attempt to export the project and then re-import it into iMovie. This might help resolve the issue.

5. **Exporting Errors**

Issue: Experiencing difficulties when attempting to export the project from iMovie.

Here's a solution:
- Make sure to check the storage space on your device. iMovie may encounter difficulties exporting the project due to insufficient storage.
- Make sure to configure the export settings accurately, including the desired file format, resolution, and compression settings.
- Consider exporting the project to a different destination or file format to determine if the issue is related to specific settings.
- If the issue continues, you may want to try exporting the project in smaller segments or reaching out to Apple Support for additional help with troubleshooting.

6. **Project Files That Are Missing or Corrupted**

Issue: Project files in iMovie have gone missing or become corrupted, resulting in the unfortunate loss of data.

Here's a solution:
- Make sure to enable automatic backups in iMovie preferences so that your projects are regularly backed up.
- Make sure to check the project library for any available backups and restore them if needed.
- In case the project files go missing or get corrupted, you can try using third-party data recovery software to retrieve them.
- It is advisable to store project files on external drives or cloud storage to enhance backup and security measures.

Tips and tricks for using iMovie effectively

Understanding the Interface

The interface of iMovie may appear overwhelming at first, but it is intentionally designed to be intuitive and user-friendly. Getting acquainted with the layout is the initial step toward becoming proficient in the software. The interface consists of several key components: the viewer, the timeline, the project media, and the toolbar. You can preview your footage and make adjustments in real time using the viewer. The timeline is the perfect tool for arranging and editing your clips, incorporating smooth transitions, and enhancing your footage with stunning effects. The project media panel houses all the media files that have been imported, such as video clips, photos, and audio. The toolbar offers convenient access to a range of editing tools, including cutting, trimming, and adding titles.

Importing and Organizing Footage

Before commencing the editing process, it is necessary to import your footage into iMovie. To accomplish this, you have the option of either clicking on the **"Import Media"** button or conveniently dragging and dropping files directly into the project media panel. After importing, you have the option to neatly organize your footage into bins or folders for convenient access.

Editing Basics

Now that you have your footage imported and organized, it's time to begin the editing process. iMovie provides a variety of essential editing tools that enable you to easily trim, split, and arrange clips on a timeline. Trimming a clip is as easy as dragging the edges in the viewer to achieve the desired duration. To split a clip, simply position the playhead at the desired location and click the **"Split Clip"** button.

Enhancing Your Content with Transitions and Effects

Adding transitions and effects can enhance the visual appeal and professionalism of your videos. iMovie provides a wide range of pre-installed transitions, including fades, dissolves, and wipes. These transitions can be effortlessly dragged and dropped between clips on the timeline. To apply an effect, just choose the clip you want and select from the options in the toolbar.

Creating Titles and Credits

Titles and credits play a crucial role in giving your audience the necessary context and information. iMovie simplifies the process of designing titles and credits, allowing you to customize fonts, colors, and animations to achieve a professional appearance. To customize the style of your titles, just click on the "Titles" button in the toolbar and select a style from the menu. Then, you can easily customize it to match your specific needs.

Enhancing Your Videos with Music and Sound Effects

Incorporating music and sound effects can significantly elevate the mood and atmosphere of your videos. iMovie offers a wide range of royalty-free music and sound effects that are readily available for use in your projects. Drag and drop the audio file onto the timeline, and adjust the volume as necessary. If you prefer, you also have the option to import your music or sound effects.

Advanced Techniques

After gaining a strong grasp of the fundamentals, you can elevate your editing skills by exploring more advanced techniques. Color correction is a technique that can enhance the overall appearance of your footage by fine-tuning the brightness, contrast, and color balance. iMovie offers a range of color correction tools, from simple exposure and saturation controls to more advanced options like color wheels and color curves. This technique is quite advanced and allows you to replace the background of a clip with a different image or video using a green screen or chroma keying. iMovie simplifies the process of creating green screen effects by providing a convenient chroma key tool. Import your green screen footage, position it over the background clip, and utilize the eyedropper tool to choose the green color for removal.

Exporting and Sharing

After completing the editing process, it's time to share your video with the world by exporting it. iMovie provides a variety of export options, allowing you to easily share your project on popular social media platforms such as YouTube, Vimeo, and Facebook. Alternatively, you can save your project as a video file directly to your computer. Make sure to select the right resolution and file format for your specific purpose before exporting.

CONCLUSION

iMovie is a user-friendly video editing app that caters to individuals who prefer a less technical editing experience. Additionally, it is an excellent choice for individuals who have already invested in the Apple ecosystem and require a straightforward video editor for app previews and movie trailers. The application offers a variety of editing features, including effects and filters. Although iMovie was designed by Apple with a focus on consumer use rather than professional use. They have another professional video editing software, which is likely the reason. It is worth noting that iMovie offers a more limited set of video editing tools compared to its competitors, and some users may find its interface less polished. The text responds to the query regarding the suitability of iMovie for editing purposes.

The application's features work smoothly and it implements video functions without any errors. iMovie offers a variety of video effects that can be applied to a clip. The software offers features such as video cropping and stabilization, transition addition, and color settings. The Video Editor is capable of editing multiple video clips at the same time, while also allowing for adjustments to audio properties. In addition, iMovie is available for both iOS and macOS. The software enables seamless importing and exporting of video projects across different versions, ensuring smooth and convenient operation. In addition, if you need to transfer the project to other Apple video editing applications, you can easily export it from iMovie.

INDEX

I

U

you can make use of the playback controls, 13

You can maximize the amount of storage space available by compressing them with HandBrake, 139

you can modify and improve the audio of a project, 43

You can organize your media by creating events, 11

you can press **Option-Command-B**, 49

You can preview a jingle or sound clip by moving the cursor, 44

You can preview your footage and make adjustments in real time, 160

you can quickly and easily drag the edges to your perusal, 7

You can quickly create a video using iMovie, 6

You can raise the level of background noise reduction by dragging the slider to the right, 54

You can replace a clip by dragging the picture, 16

you can save your project as a video file directly to your computer, 161

you can see the impact of your adjustments immediately, 2

You can see your project, 13

You can share your masterpieces straight to prominent sites, 4

you can then input the text, 8

You can upload a video from your device, 135

you can use in your film production, 7

you can use to enhance your films, 13

you can use to fine-tune your masterpiece, 2

you can use to personalize your movie to meet your preferences, 6

you do not need to save as you go., 16

You have access to a collection of music and sound clips, 44

you have the option of either clicking on the "**Import Media**" button, 160

you have the option to apply a filter to a single clip, 7

You have the option to choose from a variety of aspect ratios, 134

you have the option to neatly organize your footage into bins or folders for convenient access., 160

You may choose whether you want the footage to be played at a slow or fast rate., 8

you may create split-screen effects and use them., 13

you may give viewers the ability to fly through them, 43

You may make adjustments to the settings on your camera, 22

you may make use of the folders, 11

you may reverse clips to create one-of-a-kind visual effects., 13

You may use iMovie to bring your vision to life, 1

You may use them to make your videos more interesting, 13

You might give the impression that your movie is from the silent period, 43

you might lower the volume of the plane to improve the sound quality of your video., 53

you must first choose the files you want to import, 12

you must first click on the "**Create New**" button., 10

you must first click the **Volume button.**, 51

you must first control-click on the keyframe, 52

you must first make a movie project of your own, 16

you need to access the app., 28

you need to do is click on the "**Trim background music**" option, 9

you need to double-click the transition that you have selected., 9

you need to pick the clips you want to use. Apple's iMovie software even supports 4K video, 43

you see the green Add symbol on the screen., 68, 70

You should be aware that keyframing, 117

you should click on the blue checkmark button, 136

You should go back to iMovie and then double-click on the text section of the clip that contains the scrolling credits, 92

You should switch the camcorder to the PC Connect mode, 20

you should unplug the device, 19, 21

you want to break the picture or video, 8

You will be able to add a title at the beginning of your film project, 8

you will learn how to integrate keynote into iMovie, 144

you will need a Mac running macOS Sonoma, 109

you will need to choose the aspect ratio and resolution., 10

you will need to click on a clip that you wish to change, 8

you will need to pick the "**Clock**" button located in the bottom right corner, 8

you wish to change and split, 8

Made in the USA
Las Vegas, NV
31 May 2024

90495287R00111